The Over-Forty Society
Issues for Canada's Aging Population

Blossom T. Wigdor and David K. Foot

James Lorimer & Company, Publishers
Toronto, 1988

Cover Photo: Fourbyfive Photography

Canadian Cataloguing in Publication Data
Wigdor, Blossom T., 1924-
The Over-Forty Society
Bibliography: p.

ISBN 1-55028-087-2 (bound) ISBN 1-55028-085-6 (pbk.)

I. Aged - Canada. I. Foot, David K., 1944- II. Title.

HQ1064.C3W55 1988   305.2'6'0971   C88-094510-9

James Lorimer & Company, Publishers
Egerton Ryerson Memorial Building
35 Britain Street
Toronto, Ontario M5A 1R7

Printed and bound in Canada

5 4 3 2 1 88 89 90 91 92 93

Contents

Acknowledgments

The Programme in Gerontology of the University of Toronto provided the unique environment to carry out this work because of its multidisciplinary research in the relevant areas and its excellent support staff. We would like to thank particularly Audrey Goba for her invaluable assistance in preparing the manuscript and Anne Craik for her imaginative editing and constructive suggestions. Finally, our thanks to James Lorimer and Company, and especially to our editor, Curtis Fahey, for facilitating and encouraging this work.

Blossom T. Wigdor
David K. Foot

Preface

The aging of the Canadian population, and particularly the entry of the baby-boom generation into middle adulthood, constitutes a timely moment for publication of this book. To achieve as broad a focus as possible we have taken a multidisciplinary approach that melds two major disciplines: economics and social/behavioural science.

The book includes a brief survey of recent history and current situations as a background to understanding emerging developments. The focus is on the next 25 years, and especially on the challenges faced by individuals and society as a result of aging.

The increased life expectancy of men and women has given rise to a relatively new phenomenon: a significant increase in the very old. In addition, the aging of the large baby-boom generation will result in a dramatic increase in the middle-aged group that will move into late adulthood early in the twenty-first century. While aging imposes some inevitable trends, there still remains flexibility in making choices that will determine the nature of the society in which we live.

This book attempts to identify some of the main issues and choices that will require important decisions in the years ahead. While demographic trends occur slowly they are largely irreversible, and continued ignorance and inaction could lead to considerable social dislocation. With the large baby-boom generation now entering the over-40 society, it becomes even more imperative that some of these crucial decisions and plans be made in the near future. If they are not, the aging process will inevitably constrain the available options.

1

THE CONTEXT AND
MEANING OF AGING

Interest in growing old and in aging populations is a relatively recent phenomenon and arises from the fact that the twentieth century has seen a remarkable extension of the individual's average life expectancy at birth. This is due, in part, to the better control of infectious diseases, and to innovations in medical technology, but most of all, to our greatly improved standard of living and parallel advances in nutrition and sanitation. This extension of average life expectancy is a world-wide phenomenon, but varies considerably from country to country.

Until now, in Canada and most western industrialized countries, increases in life expectancy have occurred mainly as a result of declines in the infant mortality rates and in the number of people dying before the age of 50. As we move towards the end of the century, changes in longevity are occurring in the older age group. These increases in longevity, combined with low fertility rates and immigration trends, have changed the overall age structure of the Canadian population. This rapid aging of the population and the projected changes for the next fifty years have important implications for public policy and planning.

In analysing the impact of Canada's aging population on its economic and social institutions and policies, it is usual to define a population as aged in terms of the proportion of its population over the age of 65. However, as trends and issues related to policy involve looking ahead to what we can anticipate over the next

20 to 30 years, this book, in its discussion of some issues, will focus on the population over age 40 and thus include the transition years between what is generally seen as young and old. These middle years, the 40s and 50s, are critical, particularly in terms of employment and economic achievement as well as "life-style." The choices we make in middle age have a profound influence on the way we grow old.

DEFINITION OF "AGE" AND "OLD AGE"

The definition of old age has been changing over the years. In Canada, this is mainly due to the fact that average life expectancy at birth has increased from about 45 years, for both sexes at the turn of the twentieth century, to an average life expectancy at birth of 73 years for men and about 79.78 years for women in 1986. Because of the significant changes in life expectancy and the general well-being of many older adults we now tend to apply the definition for the word "old" to later and later chronological age.

We have also begun to realize that there are many different kinds of "old". Bernice L. Neugarten, well-known psychologist and gerontologist, in fact, has coined the term "young- old" to describe those over age 65 who are active, involved and integrated members of the community, and who continue with a life-style and activities similar to those of middle age. The "old-old" are seen as those elderly who are at an advanced age and who, because of increased frailty, may rely on others to meet some of their daily needs. Frequently, chronological ages are assigned to these categories with the "young-old" most likely 65 to 75, "middle-old" 75 to 85, and the "old-old" 85 and over. However, not everyone fits into these categories at these ages and one might become "old" earlier or later in life. In fact, Neugarten points out that we may be moving towards an "age irrelevant" society. This concept is based on a recognition both of the very individual styles of aging and of the fact that our society no longer has the same rigid view of how people of a certain age should behave.

In spite of individual differences, however, people born in the same period do share common experiences. For instance, encounters with major world events such as the Great Depression of the 1930s and World War II affect people's opportunities and possibly influence their attitudes and the way they adapt to life. A group sharing such encounters is referred to by sociologists as a "generation." Each generation comprises a set of adjacent "cohorts," groups identified by year of birth, usually separated by five- or ten-year intervals. As a sociological tool, the concept of cohorts increases our understanding of factors that influence the opportunities we have had and the social, psychological, physical and environmental factors that contribute to our choices and behaviour. Standard of living, including education, immigration patterns, rural-urban distribution, all affect the way an individual will age. Furthermore, the attrition of cohorts is important in terms of the family and social networks that help support the individual. It is well known that one's peer group or friends, as well as family peers in a household, are important to maintaining one's well-being in later life. A great deal of early work in attempting to study the aging process neglected the differences between cohorts, and therefore confused age differences with age changes.

CHANGING AGE STRUCTURE IN CANADA

Although Canada has a lower proportion of elderly than other western countries (see Table 1.1) it is nevertheless "old" by World Health Organization standards, which define an old country as one in which over 8 per cent of the population is over 65. Canada achieved that status in 1971.

In 1988, Canada has 10.7 per cent of its population over the age of 65 and by the year 2021, when the baby boomers will cross into this group, it will rise to 21 per cent. Projections about

TABLE 1.1

Percentages of Total Population Aged 65 and Over, Canada and
Selected Regions and Countries

	Selected Year	% over 65
Canada	1981	9.7
World	1980	5.8
Developed Countries	1980	11.1
Developing Countries	1980	4.0
Australia	1979	9.4
England and Wales	1980	15.1
France	1982	13.5
Sweden	1980	16.3
United States	1980	11.3
U.S.S.R.	1980	10.2

Source: Statistics Canada, 1981 Census; United Nations, Demographic Yearbook,
1981 and United States, Bureau of the Census, 1980 Census

the proportion of elderly in the population are based on demographic assumptions of future mortality rates, fertility rates (the average number of births for every woman of child-bearing age), and rates of immigration and emigration. By combining a variety of different assumptions demographers are able to develop a series of alternative population futures, or "scenarios." Table 1.2 shows projected figures of the medium growth scenario. It is based on the assumption that fertility rates will remain at about 1.66 and international migration (net gain) at about 50,000 a year.

Figure 1 illustrates the increase in the older population in another way, by separating the group into three age groups, 65 to 74, 75 to 84 and 85 and over. This delineation shows very clearly that the sector among the elderly manifesting the most rapid rate of increase is the oldest one. By the year 2001 the number of people 85 and over will have increased by 100 per cent.

TABLE 1.2

Projected Numbers and Percentages of Canadians
65 and Over, 1981-2031

	Number	% Total Pop.
1981	2,361,000	9.7
1991	3,173,300	11.8
2001	3,884,500	13.6
2011	4,544,000	15.4
2021	5,870,600	19.6
2031	7,128,400	23.9

Source: Statistics Canada, Catalogue 91-520, Population Projections for Canada,
Provinces and Territories, 1984-2006, Projection 3

FIGURE 1

Demographic Change by Elderly Age Groups
Total Projected Increase in 65+ by 2001 = 52% or 1,328,800

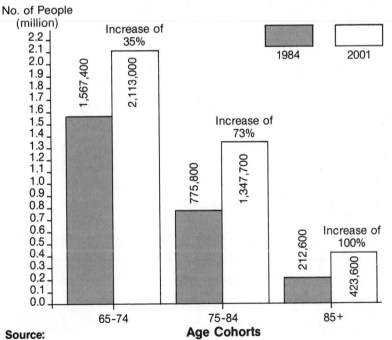

Source:
Statistics Canada. Catalogue 91-520 *Population Projections 1984-2006*

TABLE 1.3
Dependency Ratios According to the Low-growth Scenario,
Canada, Selected Years 1971-2031

Year	Dependency Ratio		
	Child	Old	Total
	0-17	65+	
1971	63.4	14.4	77.8
1981	45.2	15.6	60.8
1983	41.2	18.2	59.4
1991	37.1	21.6	58.7
2001	30.9	24.4	55.2
2011	25.3	27.4	52.7
2021	25.3	37.8	63.0
2031	25.0	51.6	76.6

Note: The dependency ratio expresses the number of people of "dependent ages"
for each 100 people of "working age."
Source: Statistics Canada, Catalogue 91-520, *Population Projections for Canada,
Provinces and Territories*, 1984-2006

The rapidly changing age structure of the population, and particularly the dramatic increase in the numbers and proportion of the very old, has important implications for many economic and social issues. Health and social services are particularly affected, as are labour markets, consumption patterns, housing, transportation and social security plans. Because there are significant differences in the needs of the younger and older old, it is very important that analyses of the data within the group aged 65 and over be studied and reported in five-year, or at least ten-year intervals.

Of major significance is the fact that the rapidly increasing older sector of the population is not predominantly part of the work-force and is largely a dependent group. The young, pre-working-age population is of course the other dependent group.

Clearly, if the structure of a population is changing, the economic burden that a society must bear in supporting its dependent groups may also change. Economists define the dependency ratio as the ratio of those members of the population who are not in paid employment for the most part, to those in the labour force. This usually refers to those under 18 years old and 65 and over. The implication is that these groups are dependent on social programmes for maintenance, or do not contribute directly to the economic productivity of the country, or both. With the changing age structure, the older age group is increasing in numbers and the group aged birth to seventeen is decreasing. Currently, because the decrease in the young-dependent ratio is greater than the increase in the elderly-dependent ratio, the total dependency ratio is decreasing and projections to the middle of the twenty-first century predict no radical changes in overall dependency ratios. (See Table 1.3).

This would seem to suggest that the general aging of the population will not be accompanied by an economic crisis. However, it is not a simple matter to reduce resources to one sector or shift resources from one sector of the population to another. Most information indicates that because the family assumes major responsibilities for social support of the pre-working-force group, the increase in the 65 and older group will generate significant costs. We still do not have accurate data on the actual dependency of the older age group. Nevertheless, we do know that there is a probability of increasing frailty, and therefore increased health and social needs as well as needs for income maintenance, among people 65 and older.

GENDER DIFFERENCES

An overview of the over-65 group, shows that women outlive men by about 7 years on the average (men 73, women 79.78). The reason for this gender difference is not known for certain, but seems to be due to a combination of genetically-based dif-

TABLE 1.4
Highest Level of Education Attained by Specific Age Groups,
Canada, 1981

Age Group	University Degree %	Post Secondary %	Grades 9-13 %	Less Than 9 %
35-44	11.8	36.2	34.2	17.8
45-54	6.9	23.0	34.1	29.9
55-64	5.1	24.0	33.6	37.2
65+	3.5	17.6	28.2	50.7

Source: Statistics Canada, Catalogue 92-827.

ferences combined with some differences in life-style. For example, the decrease in prevalence of smoking in males has reduced mortality rates in the 45 to 55 age group, while women who have not changed smoking habits show some rise in mortality due to lung cancer and cardiovascular disease (stroke). The ratio of men to women in the over-65 group is 748 to 1000 and there is a decreasing ratio of men to women with increasing age. The older the group the greater the predominance of women. There are other important gender differences in aging. On the average women's incomes are lower and most older women are single, widowed, divorced or never married. About 75 per cent of men over 65 are married and only 35 per cent of women.

EDUCATION

Educational level is an important element in understanding the general socioeconomic level and health of a group. It is therefore of some importance that the educational level of the majority of the population currently 70 and older, in Canada is approximately Grade 9, with women on the average having somewhat lower levels (see Table 1.4). However, the increasing level of education of the population generally shows that the baby-boom women have a slightly higher average number of years of schooling than men.

The above figures have important implications in terms of how dependent these groups may be in the future, and also in terms of the expectations of those people who are now young or middle-aged. The large numbers of individuals in the 35 to 65 age group may make it a slower process for the young to move into the labour force, and for individuals in the middle years to move up the economic scale.

In light of these changes in the age structure of Canada, and similar changes around the world, we as a society have become more conscious of the possibility of growing old and living in an aging population. There is anxiety and concern over this prospect because we have very negative feelings about being "old" and about old people.

ATTITUDES AND MYTHS ABOUT THE AGED

The term "ageism" was introduced by Robert L. Butler to describe a set of negative attitudes and expectations about the elderly that have the same effect as prejudicial attitudes based on race. Our fear of, and distaste for, aging manifest themselves in many ways. Entire industries, such as the cosmetic industry, have thrived because of the desire of people to stay young. Negative descriptions of aging abound in our literature and in our language. This is particularly true for women who become "crocks," "hags," "witches," and "old bags." Men change into "lechers" and "dirty old men" and, in the end, at Shakespeare's seventh stage, humankind is "sans teeth, sans eyes, sans taste, sans everything."

There are also a number of myths about aging. The first is that conclusions about the functioning of an individual at a particular time can be made based on chronological age alone. In fact, individuals age at different rates, and older individuals are extremely heterogeneous due to different life experiences super-imposed on their genetic and physical differences.

A second myth is that all old people lose their intellectual capacities and become "senile." In fact, although there is some change in the efficiency of mental functioning in later life, most individuals in reasonable health maintain their mental abilities. The term "senility" should be discarded completely because it implies a significant loss of mental capacity with advanced age. Senile dementia is a degenerative neurological disease that at-tacks 5 to 15 per cent of the population over age 65, the incidence of which increases over the age of 85 to 20 to 36 per cent. (Different figures arise due to different definitions and methods of assessing individuals.) Senile dementia is primarily due to Alzheimer's Disease or stroke, and is not a part of the aging process itself.

A third myth is that older people are unproductive. Although the participation of older people in the paid labour force goes down dramatically after the age of 65 these people still remain productive in many ways. One has only to look to Pablo Cassels, who continued to play the cello and compose until he was in his nineties; Pablo Picasso, Charlie Chaplin, Leopold Stokowski, Somerset Maugham, Georgia O'Keefe, Grandma Moses, Bertrand Russell and many others who remained productive until very advanced age. Many older people continue to work and con-tribute by helping raise grandchildren, doing volunteer work in the community or simply being community members and economic consumers pursuing personal and family interests. Furthermore, older workers can be as productive as younger workers, particularly in jobs where experience is important, or where they continue in familiar tasks. They have less absen-teeism, make fewer errors and show less turnover than younger workers.

A fourth myth is that older people cannot learn. A well-known saying is that "you cannot teach an old dog new tricks." In fact, research shows that older individuals, whether you consider older 45 or 85, can learn new information and new skills. The time required to learn, the relevance of the information or skill, the motivation of the individual and the setting for learning may vary or change somewhat, but the ability to learn remains. Everyday life illustrates this point. Many elderly change neighbourhoods, or find it necessary to shop in a new supermarket. They learn very quickly how to live in the new environment. It is true their past experience will be a help but, in fact, learning is the ability to adapt past knowledge to a new situation. One of the oldest graduates of the University of Toronto undergraduate programme was 92, and many seniors take courses in undergraduate programmes throughout Canada and compete successfully with their younger classmates, although they may not carry the same academic load at any one time.

One of the most general characteristics of the aging process in the human being is a tendency for there to be a general slowing in the time it takes to react to a stimulus or event. For example, a driver over age 70 is likely to take longer to apply the brakes for an emergency stop than a driver of 25. This affects most functions, physical and mental. However, there are marked individual variations in the degree of change over time, and the effect on particular functions may not be significant. Recent studies indicate that the performance of older individuals can be improved by training, and this includes speed of response. Therefore, some rethinking about this issue will have to take place.

A fifth myth is that the elderly are asexual. In fact, the older person continues to be capable of, and interested in, sexual activity until very old age unless ill health intervenes. The strength of the sex drive may diminish, but the need for love, affection and physical contact remains. Sexual behaviour in later life will depend a great deal on what an individual's sexual behaviour pattern was like in earlier years. Individuals vary considerably throughout life in terms of the amount of interest in sex, the frequency of sexual intercourse, the type of sexual expression and so on. In addition, social conditions such as lack of sexual partners due to widowhood, and the social attitudes of a particular generation, may influence sexual behaviour in later life. Negative attitudes about sexual expression among the elderly often act as a barrier to sexual expression. Feelings of shame, or a sense of inappropriateness, can easily inhibit the fulfillment of sexual needs. Consider, for example, the fact that few homes for the aged or nursing homes make any provision for privacy. If residents of such institutions make attempts to come together to express affection or sexual need, this is often felt to be a "problem." Alex Comfort has likened sexuality and aging to riding a bicycle in that, one, you have to be in reasonably good health, two, you cannot feel foolish doing it and three, you must have a bicycle.

The sixth myth is that all older people are rigid and resist change. This characteristic is seen as a personality trait and somehow tied to the inability to learn or change, as well as to the innate conservatism of older people. In fact, older people do change and they do not undergo significant personality change. There is evidence that they may become more cautious about making changes because of increased risk and less potential return. For example, it is easier to change jobs at 25 than at 55. You may take a financial loss more easily at an earlier age because you have a greater chance of recouping that loss. It has also been suggested that the tendency to continue to solve problems in familiar ways may be due to decreased mental capacity and physical energy. But in fact, there is always a tendency to solve new problems, or deal with everyday situations, in terms of past experience and solutions. There has to be significant reward to seek new solutions.

The seventh myth is that of tranquillity. It is frequently assumed that reaching a specific chronological age transforms one into a calm person with no problems and an air of complete contentment — a notion that conforms with the stereotypical image of a benevolent, smiling, cookie-baking grandmother. In fact, old age carries with it many changes, often involving losses, and most individuals tend to cope with these reasonably well, but not without stress and crises. Eric Erickson argues that in the last stage of life people should achieve a state of "integrity" in which review of the past helps them reconcile earlier goals with present achievements and thus results in a reasonable feeling of satisfaction. Thus, for some people this state of equilibrium may come, but it is usual only very late in life.

Other myths suggest that the elderly are sick, poor, irritable, querulous and garrulous. The latter three characteristics relate to personality and it has already been pointed out that there are no really significant personality changes during later life. Nevertheless, if life is heavily weighted with unhappy developments, we might quite realistically become dissatisfied. In fact, the elderly are a group with the entire range of personal characteristics found in the population at large.

Most elderly in the community when surveyed report themselves in fair to good, or excellent, health and most do not report income to be their greatest worry. Nevertheless, about 75 per cent of those over age 65 have some chronic medical condition that may not interfere with their activities of daily living, but may require health care and a change in life-style. Yet, we must be very careful not to generalize about the medical problems of the older adult population. Indeed, in this respect as in others, the older age group is more heterogeneous than younger age groups, since how a person ages is affected by the interaction of genetic heritage, life-style and experience.

The power of these myths is that they do not only influence the social policies that will be developed, but also the attitudes of those who interact with the elderly on either a social or professional level. Furthermore, the elderly who have been raised in this myth-ridden society are liable to hold similar views about aging and the old. These beliefs then often lead to anxiety about aging and even to "self-fulfilling prophecies." They also tend to make the elderly often accept a lower quality of life than they can realistically aspire to. Their life situation often demands a lowering of standards as society attempts to make the elderly "invisible."

Although these negative beliefs are very widely held, there is considerable evidence that it is also a myth that we abandon our elderly. Studies have shown that North American families do not abandon their elderly, and most live within a fifteen minute drive of at least one child or, in the case of the childless, of one other kin such as a sibling. Furthermore, a great deal of care is given to the elderly by adult children.

There has been a widespread belief in western cultures that there was a "golden age" when the elderly were highly respected and that only in modern society have they been devalued. But there is no strong evidence to support this view. As already noted, the average life expectancy at birth, at the turn of the 20th century, was about 45 years of age. Until recently, most individuals, therefore, died at a relatively early age. Those who did survive longer were likely to be rich and of high status, and thus respected for their power rather than for their advanced years. Furthermore, agricultural societies tended to pass land from "heads" of families, who were men, to the eldest son, and the surviving widow was often relegated to a secondary role in the household. The advent of industrialization also brought with it a sick and impoverished group who could not continue to work, and "almshouses," the predecessors of homes for the aged, came into being mainly for the old. In medieval Europe there were many cases of parents suing children for support. It is true that various cultures have had different degrees of respect for the elderly; for example, Japanese and Chinese cultures, with religions based on ancestor worship, traditionally showed respect for their elderly in their languages and customs. However, with new social pressures there is some evidence of change in the status of the elderly even in these cultures. Current economic pressures in some countries are responsible for an increased effort to maintain intergenerational ties in order to keep grandparents available for child care or to share housing.

In general, "old age" was not endowed in the past with a very positive image, although the fact that there were few old may have given rise to feelings of awe or fear. After all, would a Biblical commandment to "honour thy father and thy mother" have been necessary if this were such a natural inclination?

Today we face an aging population. If the needs of this population are to be met, there will have to be some shift in social values as well as the development of new public policies. More individuals will face aging and old age as a personal reality. One scholar has claimed that, with better understanding of chronic diseases, we will face this longer life healthier and more satisfied, and the end of life will be marked by a relatively short terminal illness or decline. This view is the subject of controversy and others argue that aging may bring new chronic medical problems. However, as individuals we may have choices to fashion a life-style that will make aging easier. Moreover, individuals who are healthier and better educated are going to be more demanding of a social and physical environment better suited to their needs.

SOCIAL POLICY AND PUBLIC POLICY LINKS

As the foregoing indicates, the aging of individuals and of the population as a whole is the result of a complex interaction of factors that have implications for the functional well-being of individuals, and how they contribute to society. At the same time, the values a society holds collectively determine the kind of society it creates for its citizens.

The issues raised in this book examine trends and make inferences about the impact of some of these factors on both economic and social policy. The changing age structure of our population will present us with fundamental choices. Our social values tend to be those of a welfare state where the primary concerns are need and equity. Yet, we also operate in a market economy and therefore the generation and allocation of resources are fundamental issues. Looking from the past and present to the future is a difficult and sometimes hazardous task. However, the analysis in the following chapters should indicate both the need for planning and the options to be considered in the planning process.

2

LABOUR MARKET ISSUES

As individuals enter the over-40 age groups, one of their most important concerns centres on current and future employment status, since it determines not only income but also self-esteem. Is it now or never as far as a career change is concerned? Will aging lead to higher or lower real incomes? What are the opportunities for promotion, or mobility to other employers, for the older worker? What are the chances of being laid off or otherwise released and, if it occurs, what are the probabilities of being hired elsewhere? Is early retirement a good idea? What is the situation regarding mandatory retirement and what opportunities, if any, exist for part-time employment beyond the mandatory retirement age? These are very important questions that raise equally important issues both for the individual and for society.

Not only is Canada's population aging, but so is its labour force. However, this is a relatively recent phenomenon. Over the 1960s and 1970s the labour force became younger and younger as wave after wave of baby boomers entered the labour market. The first baby boomers, born in 1947, became of labour-force age in 1962 and thereafter, for an entire generation of 20 years, annual growth of the labour force in Canada exceeded 3 per cent — well above all other countries in the western world. Over the 1960s the only other country to exceed 2.5 per cent average annual growth was Australia, while over the 1970s the closest country with average annual growth, still almost .5 per cent below that of Canada, was the United States. This performance adequately mirrors the extent and magnitude of the baby boom in Canada.

Then came the 1980s. Over the first half of the decade, labour-force growth fell to an annual average of 1.8 per cent — almost one half of the growth over the previous two decades. And while this period encompassed the most severe economic downturn in Canada since the depression of the 1930s, the declining growth reflected far more than short-term macro-economic performance; it signalled the beginning of an era of much slower labour-force growth in Canada for the remainder of the century. New entrants to the labour force were coming from the much smaller "baby-bust" generation (born between 1967 and 1979) and the children of the baby boomers — the so-called echo effect of the 1980s — will not start entering the Canadian labour force until the turn of the century. Even this impact will not be large by historical standards.

As with the population, a slower growing labour force means an aging labour force. This creates both new opportunities and new challenges. Slower growth means fewer new people to be employed. Job creation, the watchword of economic policies of all governments in Canada over the 1960s and 1970s, will have a much lower profile over the late 1980s and 1990s. Demographic developments will no longer push unemployment rates upward, but rather will contribute to lowering rates. However, the reduced numbers of new entrants will mean a scarcity of new skills and ideas, and considerably less flexibility in the management of human resources. In an era of rapidly changing technology, education depreciates with the passage of time, so an aging labour force could mean a labour force potentially *less* able to handle technological change. Moreover, older workers, with the family and financial commitment that age brings, are generally less mobile than younger workers over geographical regions, industries and occupations. In addition, they usually become increasingly specialized in a particular occupation or industry and, with depreciating education, less able to make the transition to other occupations or industries where growth and prospects are better.

Increased age and specialization do have advantages. It is widely recognized that labour-market experience is an asset for which there can be few, if any, substitutes. Increasing experience is often associated with increasing maturity, especially for younger workers, and increasing knowledge of an organization's products, personalities, problems and politics. This enhances the employee's ability to contribute successfully to the organization, presumably increasing productivity.

There is considerable debate on when, if ever, an individual's productivity peaks. Certainly the combination of gradually depreciating educational skills, and possible changes in cognitive skills suggests that a maximum may well be reached over an employee's working lifetime. But there are many other factors that are also relevant. Motivation is influenced by personal relationships and corporate culture. Changes in personnel and the corporate reward systems can have noticeable effects on productivity, and these may vary at different points in a person's life. Even experience may play a role in shaping productivity as efficiency replaces energy as the dominating force behind labour-market activity.

Sooner or later, however, aging must affect work performance. This can arise in many ways, from physical disabilities (which may even be caused by the work environment), to some declining cognitive capabilities. The recognition of these effects is reflected in the institution of retirement from the active or paid labour force, although non-paid work activity may well continue into an individual's later years. Of course, this point is reached by different individuals at a wide variety of ages, which is why the choice of "the" retirement age is such a contentious issue in current policy debates.

These latter issues are rapidly becoming more important in Canada. With the baby-boom generation now completely absorbed into the Canadian labour force, the focus is rapidly changing from one of labour surplus — the dominant characteristic of the 1960s and 1970s — to one of labour scarcity. The social concern with job creation is gradually being replaced by an emerging recognition of the importance of human resource planning. One of the main challenges of the 1990s will lie in achieving the maximum productivity from a slower-growing and aging labour force.

Such a general and far-reaching issue can only be addressed successfully if confronted at the individual level. Individual organizations working with individual employees, or employee groups, will need to explore the most appropriate ways to generate increases in productivity from older workers. Buoyed by the increasing experience in this labour force, organizations will have to focus on ways to offset depreciating educational skills, encourage mobility, ease career crises, stimulate motivation and retirement. The focus of the labour market in Canada is moving from the problems of the younger workers — youth unemployment, for example — to the problems of the mature and older workers. This is the logical result of Canadian demographic developments, and sets the scene for the issues to be discussed in this chapter.

LABOUR FORCE CHARACTERISTICS

By 1986 the Canadian labour force numbered almost thirteen million people. This means that approximately two of every three people of working age were seeking employment. Over 90 per cent were employed in either full-time or part-time positions, the latter accounting for approximately 15 per cent of all jobs. Not surprisingly, given demographic developments, by far the majority of the labour force was under age 40. For every person over age 40 in the labour force in 1986, there were approximately two younger people.

Participation and performance within the labour market varies notably over the age groups. Almost 70 per cent of the youth (aged 15 to 24) were seeking work, while 84 per cent of those aged 25 to 44 were in the labour force. However, only 65 per cent of those aged 45 to 64 and, a considerably lower 7 per cent of those aged 65 and over, considered themselves to be in the paid labour force. These proportions vary by gender, with female labour force participation rates, despite substantial increases over the previous decade, still below male participation rates and female unemployment rates generally above male unemployment rates. These are summarized in Table 2.1.

Of particular interest are the labour market characteristics of older workers. Labour force participation drops substantially in the older age groups for both men and women. For example, between the 45 to 54, and the 55 to 64 age groups for men, the participation rate falls from 91.5 to 68.5 per cent, while for women it falls from 60.7 to 33.4 per cent. This reflects the phenomenon of "early" retirement — that is, retirement prior to the age of 65. More detailed data indicate that this phenomenon currently becomes most apparent around the middle fifties, especially for men. By age 64 approximately 50 per cent of men and 20 per cent of women are in the labour force. One year later these figures have been approximately halved.

It is, nonetheless, important to note that a number of older Canadians continue to seek employment beyond age 65. In total, 179,000 of over 2.5 million people were in this category of which the majority were aged 65 to 69 (61.5 per cent) and were male (71 per cent). Almost all were employed, two out of three in full-time positions. The numbers in the older labour force were largely unchanged over the previous decade in spite of a significant increase in the number of elderly over the period. In 1976, 176,000 of 1.86 million older Canadians sought employment. A peak occurred in 1984 when 192,000 of 2.36 million older Canadians sought employment. Since then the participation rate has declined from 7.7 to 7.1 per cent in this age group.

The future is largely, although not entirely, predetermined by these demographic characteristics. Over the decade of the 1990s the leading edge of the baby-boom generation gradually enters the over-40 age groups. Someone born in 1947 reaches age 40 in 1987, and age 60 in 2007. The peak of the baby boom born in 1961 enters the over-40 age groups in 2001, and the over-60 age groups twenty years later. All of this means that the labour-force growth of the over-40 age group can be expected to expand dramatically over the foreseeable future. While continuation of the trends to early retirement, and hence lower participation rates, could ameliorate these trends somewhat, they might be off-

TABLE 2.1

Labour Force Characteristics, Canada, 1986

Age/Gender Group	Working Age	Labour Force	Employment Rate	Partici-pation	Employment Rate
Males:	Mi	llions	%	%	%
15-24	2.11	1.51	1.26	71.5	16.5
25-44	4.01	3.80	3.48	94.6	8.3
45-64	2.37	1.92	1.79	80.7	6.5
65+	1.08	0.13	0.12	11.7	N.A.
Total	9.57	7.36	6.65	76.7	9.4
Females:					
15-24	2.05	1.34	1.16	65.6	13.8
25-44	4.08	2.96	2.69	72.6	9.3
45-64	2.46	1.17	1.08	47.4	7.3
65+	1.43	0.05	0.05	3.7	N.A.
Total	10.02	5.52	4.98	55.1	9.9
Both Sexes:					
Total	19.59	12.88	11.63	65.7	9.6

Source: Statistics Canada, *The Labour Force*, December 1986

set by increasing life expectancy and certainly are unlikely to alter substantially the basic demographic facts — namely, an ever larger proportion of the Canadian labour force will be entering the over-40 age groups, and this will generate numerous challenges and opportunities.

BLOCKED CAREER PATHS

For the youngest members of this older labour force — the middle-aged workers — the first major issue that is likely to emerge is the issue of blocked career paths. This results not only from the sheer size of the baby-boom generation, with the resulting intensified competition for better jobs, but also from the decreasing numbers of opportunities inherently available in hierarchial or pyramidal corporate structures. The results are predictable; increasing worker dissatisfaction in the swollen ranks of cohorts of middle-aged workers as opportunites for advancement appear more limited than in the past. It should not be surprising if this results in lower productivity among these dissatisfied workers.

Under such conditions Michael Driver has suggested a need for workers to reorient and adjust to the concept of "spiralling" career paths, rather than "linear" career paths; that is, a career profile that includes a mixture of lateral and vertical moves during a career, rather than comprising purely promotional or vertical advancements. Judging success solely in terms of the latter types of position changes — changes that move the employee towards the peak of the pyramidal organizational structure — is destined to lead to disappointment and dissatisfaction.

A spiralling career culture requires a fundamental shift in social values. It places heavy demands on the retraining of older workers to facilitate their transition to different occupations or, at least, different tasks in the same general occupation. It may also require a greater encouragement of inter-organizational transfers, including not only executive, but management and worker interchanges with other organizations. Such adjustments will place a heavy emphasis on human resource planning within the corporate structure. It must take place at all levels where career blocking is likely to be a reality. To be successful it must be reflected in remuneration or benefit packages, including a salary increase for a lateral move, and liberal educational leaves with appropriate financial incentives to "reward" the employee who is responding individually to these environmental changes. This implies that hierarchial pay structures will have to be dismantled to accommodate the laterally moving employee who may well be earning more than his or her boss. It also implies that the era of the "generalist" is likely returning. To remain motivated and productive, the typical employee will have to have experienced a number of different positions and, likely, regions, industries and occupations over a working life, rather than pursuing increased specialization within one organization.

These changes could also have a "payoff" later in retirement since the "spiralling" employee will have had a greater chance to have been exposed to different work environments and colleagues, and hence a greater variety of potential interests and opportunities for human interaction in retirement. This benefit may appear tenuous now, but with increasing life expectancy and improved health, any changes that can contribute to active and challenging retirement years are likely to prove increasingly beneficial.

EARLY RETIREMENT

Once in their fifties many employees contemplate the possibility of early retirement. Many writers have noted that such a decision is mainly determined by health status and, especially, pension or income considerations. Employees are much more likely to choose early retirement if they are covered by adequate and flexible pension provisions. The total income in retirement from all sources is the prime determinant of the decision. In this regard "golden handshake" policies can be influential in reaching the decision to take early retirement.

With the Canada/Quebec Pension Plan (C/QPP) having been established in 1966, increasing numbers of retiring employees now have at least some access to pension income. Moreover, the recently introduced flexible retirement option, which permits a contributor to retire at any age between 55 and 75, is likely to provide further opportunities to those for whom early retirement is a viable alternative. Currently, a contributor who retires at age 55 would receive 70 per cent of full eligible benefits at age 65 under the C/QPP, and these benefits would increase by 3 per cent for each additional year that the retirement decision is postponed up to a maximum 130 per cent at age 75. Thus, a contributor who chooses to wait until age 75 to retire will have contributed 20 more years to the plan compared to a retiree at age 55, and thus have contributed to the increased benefits, which will also be received over a shorter remaining lifetime. It is in this way that the new provisions can be actuarially justified.

In addition, the Conference Board of Canada has estimated that, for the economy as a whole, approximately one in two employees works for employers with pension plans. These employees receive additional benefits from plans with their employers. However, the pension literature is replete with documentation of the variety and complexity of these plans, most of which do not have formal flexible retirement provisions. In these cases, one form of "golden handshake" is the employer's informal "adjustment" to the pension provisions to facilitate an early retirement decision. The decision and power rests predominantly with the employer rather than with the employee.

A further, often debated, issue with respect to these plans is their portability — the opportunity for employees to transfer the pension obligations of employer plans to different employment settings and hence to different employers. This is complicated not only by the wide variety of different employer plans with the associated actuarial complexities, but also by an apparent lack of commitment or capability on behalf of both private and public sectors to resolve the issue. Unfortunately, the issue cannot be expected to disappear. On the contrary, as more people reach retirement age, pension issues are likely to increase in importance. And, if the spiralling career path becomes more commonplace, the likelihood that an employee will have had more than one employer increases significantly and thus increases the magnitude of the problem.

The trend towards early retirement is reflected in the decreasing labour force participation rates in the older age groups, especially the 55 to 64 age group. This rate has fallen from around 77 per cent in 1977 to 68.5 per cent a decade later. The female rate has remained around 33 per cent, thus reflecting an offsetting of the trend towards early retirement by a trend towards greater female participation in the labour force. Individual year data (not shown) indicate that the downward trend is apparent for all ages in this age group, but especially for those aged 59 and up. As noted previously, by age 64 approximately 50 per cent of men and 20 per cent of women remain in the Canadian labour force. One year later these figures are almost halved.

MANDATORY RETIREMENT

The dramatic decline in labour force participation rates at age 65 in Canada reflects the phenomenon of mandatory retirement, which has been traditionally located at this age. Until recently, the employee had few if any opportunities, let alone rights, to challenge the employer's prerogative in this decision. There were, however, exceptions. Both the provinces of Manitoba and Quebec through court decisions and legislation effectively abolished mandatory retirement in the middle to late 1970s. More recently, the passing of the Canadian *Charter of Rights and Freedoms* by federal legislation has provided a medium for the employee to challenge this employers' prerogative. The results are still largely uncertain, at least to the non-legal community, as each individual case is decided on its individual merits, and decisions are appealed to higher courts. No nationwide general trends have as yet emerged, although undoubtedly it is fair to conclude that the pressures are to reduce the stringent mandatory retirement provisions of employer-specific pension plans and of employment in general.

The wisdom of such a move is subject to considerable controversy and debate. Economists Morley Gunderson and James Pesando have argued that the mandatory retirement provision acts as a humane industrial relations policy. Employers are willing to maintain employees whose productivity does not match their salary on the payroll for a limited period at the end of their career, if they know for certain that the employee will be retired at a specified time. The alternative, argue the authors, is for the continual monitoring of employees' productivity — an exercise that, they argue, is both costly and demeaning. In addition, dismissal procedures would have to be established for employees who do not meet the productivity criteria, and, so as not to be age discriminatory, these procedures would have to be applied to all employees. Such dismissals may have profound negative effects on employees entering retirement, whereas the existence of mandatory retirement permits the employee to enter retirement with "grace and dignity."

Another argument in favour of mandatory retirement is that Canadian society has an obligation to maintain mandatory retirement to provide jobs for the massive baby-boom generation currently in their twenties and thirties. According to this view the "rights" of these workers to a challenging job need to be balanced against the "rights" of the older workers, and relatively higher unemployment rates for this generation is *prima-facie* evidence that their rights are being violated. Although this is a somewhat extreme position, mandatory retirement among older workers can create opportunities that facilitate the upward (and even lateral) mobility for younger workers, which will become increasingly necessary in the Canadian labour market if opportunity, motivation and productivity are to be maintained, let alone enhanced.

The opponents of mandatory retirement focus on its arbitrariness. They argue that there is nothing inherent in age 65 to justify its choice as *the* age of retirement in the first place, and that with improving general health and life expectancy among older Canadians this age is becoming increasingly irrelevant as an indicator of productivity. Moreover, it is likely that human productivity, like capital productivity, declines gradually and not, as economist John Maynard Keynes noted, as a "one horse shay." Finally, the choice of age 65 as the mandatory retirement age is arbitrary with respect to the individual employee, because health and the many other personal characteristics that contribute to productivity performance vary so much across individuals. Hence, opponents of mandatory retirement argue that retirement decisions should be administered on an individual basis. They tend to be optimistic about the capabilities of the existing industrial relations mechanisms to handle the monitoring and dismissal procedures. Where possible, these would become part of a collective agreement, and hence subject to input from both employers and employees.

Needless to say, this is a simplification of an extremely complex issue. It is an issue, however, that seems to be receiving considerably more attention in the courts than in the industrial relations bargaining system. This is because recent trends have been dominantly towards earlier, rather than later, retirement. Consequently, most employees and employee groups have been mainly concerned with fighting for early retirement provisions in labour contracts, rather than for resolving the issue of mandatory retirement. Instead, mandatory retirement provisions are being fought in the courts.

This could well change in the future. As Canadians remain healthy and alive for longer and longer, so they may wish to remain in paid employment longer and longer. For example, an average life expectancy of 60 years would imply a high probability of death before retirement, while a life expectancy of 70 years implies an average of 5 years of retirement, or approximately 10 per cent of an average working lifespan (of 15 to 64). A life expectancy of 80 years implies an average of 15 years of retirement, or approximately 30 per cent of an average working lifespan if the retirement age is specified at 65. To obtain a 10 per cent retirement ratio would require an increase in the age of retirement to approximately 74 years; even a 20 per cent retirement ratio would require an increase in the retirement age to 69.

Another argument advanced for extending the age of retirement focuses on dependency ratios. According to this argument, in a country like Canada, which has such a quantitatively large baby-boom generation, society will have difficulty paying for the support of the elderly in the future. Such support includes not only pension benefits but also health, social services and housing services, among other things. Since the following generations are quantitatively so much smaller, these financing costs associated with an elderly baby-boom generation will impose a heavy burden on them, and extending the retirement age would help reduce this burden by increasing the taxable base and reducing the benefits as these people remain in employment longer. However, calculations have shown that since the first baby boomers born in 1947 do not reach age 65 until the year 2012, the effect will not likely be felt for a quarter of a century. More important, the financial pressures, although increasing at that time, are likely to be relatively moderate. This, therefore, would seem to be a less cogent argument for changing the retirement age.

The survey of the Conference Board of Canada mentioned above indicated that approximately one-quarter of all employees retire at age 65. This is largely confirmed in the statistics on labour force participation, which declines substantially at that age. The remainder either die, become unemployed or retire early as a result of poor health or early retirement provisions in their pensions. A small percentage (4 per cent in the survey) work beyond their 65th birthday. As noted previously, approximately

7 per cent of all Canadians currently over age 65, and only 4 per cent of those over age 70, remain in the labour force.

In summary, mandatory retirement remains a contentious issue for older workers, with arguments advanced both for its retention and its abolishment. The issue is currently being fought in the courts rather than in the industrial relations system and no general trends have yet emerged. Manitoba, Quebec and New Brunswick have made changes in their provincial laws to abolish mandatory retirement at age 65. The pressures are clearly for some relaxation in the retirement provisions, either towards flexible retirement or towards a higher or no general retirement age. This is likely to remain an important issue for older workers.

PART-TIME EMPLOYMENT

An alternative to both flexible and mandatory retirement is part-time retirement, or its converse of part-time employment. In this way the older worker could gradually exit from the labour force. For example, an employee might work full-time up to age 55 and then the equivalent of four days a week (80 per cent time) between ages 55 and 59, 3 days a week (60 per cent) between ages 60 and 64, 2 days a week (40 per cent) between ages 65 and 69 and, finally, 1 day a week (20 per cent) between ages 70 and 75. This could be accomplished by working fewer days, or by working fewer hours in a day, or by some combination of the two. Undoubtedly, the role played by the employee in the organization would change over this period, but there would be adequate time to adjust to these changes. Such a schedule would assure more continuity in an organization's employees, and provide older workers with the opportunity to transfer their experience to younger employees. This is often not the case when an employee leaves the organization entirely from a full-time position. Moreover, it would also provide the opportunity to exit the organization and labour force with "grace and dignity," a provision that is less likely to be achievable with abolished mandatory retirement.

This option does not appear to be receiving the attention it likely deserves. Although there has been a trend towards increased part-time employment in the economy, it remains true that only about 10 per cent of all part-time jobs are held by those aged 55 and over and this percentage has not been increasing. For the 65 and over group the figure is less than 3.5 per cent. The dominant group of part-time employees are youth, who currently account for over 40 per cent of all part-time employees. Women aged 25 to 44 account for a further 30 per cent. Thus, the part-time employment (or retirement) option is being taken up by the youth and younger women and there is little evidence of its being considered by older workers. It might be argued that women aged 55 to 64 are considering the option — one-quarter of them are employed in part-time jobs — but this is still virtually no higher than the female average. Not surprisingly, the percentages are higher for older workers. Thirty per cent of all men and 45 per cent of all women employees aged 65 and over have part-time positions, but this is still a small fraction of the total number of part-time employees.

ADAPTATION TO RETIREMENT

Retirement constitutes a withdrawal from the labour force. It may be abrupt or gradual, forced or voluntary. There are many reasons why an individual chooses to retire. Layoffs and unemployment or poor health may force retirement, adequate pensions may facilitate retirement, "golden handshakes" may induce retirement, but the desire, and perhaps need, for more leisure time is likely to also be a determining factor. It is the use of this increased leisure time that is the key to a successful transition and adaption to the retired life-style.

Perhaps the most important factor influencing this successful transition is health status. Those in poor health seldom find the transition easy. Quite often their work provided an opportunity to "forget" their ill-health or to share their problems with fellow workers. Upon retirement neither of these options is available and the problem must be borne entirely by the "patient." This can be emotionally as well as physically debilitating, and certainly does not contribute to a successful transition or adaption to the retired life-style.

A second important factor in this process is income. Economic security is a major concern of the elderly, especially elderly women who, on average, live longer and may not have comparable access to pension income as men. However, this concern is not unique to the elderly. Adequate and guaranteed incomes can certainly reduce anxieties that can contribute to a successful retirement. But it can contribute to success throughout the life cycle and not just in retirement.

Probably a unique factor to retirees is the possible loss of self-worth or a feeling of no longer contributing to society that often accompanies the termination of paid employment. This effect is, on average, likely to be more devastating in the event of an abrupt exit from the labour force compared to a gradual exit or a planned exit. In this case, the part-time or mandatory retirement options likely offer the better means for the transition into retirement than the no-mandatory-retirement option.

A further loss in retirement can be the lost "socialization" of the work environment. Employment generally brings an employee into close contact with fellow workers, a contact that may well be enriched by the feeling of "team" membership. This is lost almost completely upon retirement. Even if former colleagues are maintained as friends, the environment within which the contacts occur has been unalterably changed. To some this will prove a decided asset, but to many it will not. And for those who lose contact with their former colleagues, in one way or another, their opportunities for socialization are significantly reduced.

It is often claimed that a "key" to successful retirement is a broad set of interests or activities. While this is largely an individual characteristic, it may be influenced by the previous work environment. A person who has experienced more positions is likely to have been exposed to more potential interests and activities that may be further developed in retirement. They are also more likely to have a larger potential pool of friends to draw on for social interaction. In this way the spiralling career path outlined in this chapter may contribute to increased success in adapting to retirement.

A successful retirement is, undoubtedly, the key to the post-labour market life for most people. This fact, although so often considered to be "in the future," requires that current employees pay careful attention to this issue *during* their working lives. In this way, they can plan for a successful transition and adaption to retirement.

3

PENSIONS AND INCOME MAINTENANCE

Population aging means more people in retirement. As noted in the previous chapter, retirement from the paid labour force is determined to a large extent by the availability of sufficient income for the individual (or couple) in their retirement years. Pensions provide the dominant, but not the only, means of income support to Canadians in retirement. Investment earnings, primarily bank interest, account for a significant (one-fifth) share, but recent data indicate that 42 per cent of all seniors receive no investment income whatsoever, and three in five receive $1,000 or less from this source. The aging of the population can be expected to place greater emphasis and scrutiny on these income sources in the years ahead, although the major pressures will not be experienced until the baby boom reaches the retirement ages starting in the second decade of the twenty-first century. But, as noted below, careful planning cannot be delayed until then.

Pension plans, by far the most important income source for the elderly, have been designed to provide economic security or support at the time when individuals can no longer always adequately provide for themselves — upon retirement from regular paid employment. There are many different forms of pension plans reflecting, in part, different objectives and, in part, different ways of collecting and disbursing monies through the plan.

Currently in Canada there are two main government plans that provide substantial income support (almost one-half of the total) for those in retirement — the Old Age Security (OAS) programme and the Canada/Quebec Pension Plan (C/QPP). There are other programmes that are integrated with these two plans, such as the Guaranteed Income Supplement (GIS) and the Spouse's Allowance (SA), which are income-tested. In addition, some of the provinces provide supplementary programmes to the elderly or those in financial need who can no longer work. There is also a myriad of private and self-funded pension plans for those who are eligible. This chapter provides a brief review of current pension arrangements in Canada and concludes with a review of outstanding pension issues that affect both the individual and society.

PENSION DEFINITIONS

Pensions are, usually regular, financial payments that are made as a result of government legislation to the individual on the attainment of a specified age. They may be limited to individuals with low incomes. They also include payments arising from government legislation or employer plans that relate to years of employment and salaries received. This definition distinguishes pensions from self-directed retirement savings plans, although these will be considered later in the chapter.

It is apparent that a pension plan has at least two distinct dimensions. First, it is designed to provide income security for those who receive little family support, or who find themselves with insufficient financial resources through private pension or personal savings plans. Second there is income replacement (or maintenance), which is focused on offsetting or ameliorating the reduction in income that most employees experience upon retirement. It is useful to keep the two objectives clearly in mind when discussing pension issues. Obviously, the first logically precedes the second in that a basic minimum pension is required before consideration can be given to a "top up" to cover income replacement. Nonetheless, both are based on the presumption that the individual has "retired" from regular paid employment and, therefore, can no longer obtain adequate financial resources through paid employment. It is in this sense that the word pensions is used.

In general, pension plans collect contributions from people at work and pay benefits or pensions to those who withdraw from the labour force because of advanced age. Contributions may be made by both employee and employer and are usually related to the earnings of the employee. In this sense, general income taxes, which are based on earnings and are used to pay income support to the needy elderly under government legislation, may qualify as pensions. In the more usual case, where a defined plan is in force, the amount of the pension is determined either by the amount of money to the employee's credit at retirement or by some formula relating the pension to the employment and earnings history of the employee. The former are called defined contribution plans while the latter are referred to as formula or defined benefit plans. Another, less common, pension plan is the level payment benefit plan in which payments are identical to every retired member. In addition to the pension payments, death benefits may be paid to heirs of pension plan members. These general characteristics of pension plans apply whether the sponsor of the plan is a government or a private organization. Sponsors are those organizations responsible for the administration of the plan, and ultimately for its solvency, and may include governments (at all levels), employers, trade unions, co-operative societies, insurance companies and other financial intermediary organizations. Employer-sponsored plans may be trusteed or insured depending on whether the facilities for accumulation and disbursement of pension monies are provided by a trust (or a co-operative) or an insurance company.

The operation of a pension plan can be on a pay-as-you-go or on a funded basis. Under a pay-as-you-go operation benefits are paid out of the current revenues of the sponsor. For governments, these revenues come from the usual fiscal sources while the expenses appear under general operating expenses. Similarly, for other organizations, they usually appear as separate items in the operating budget statements. Under a funded operation a dedicated fund is established into which all contributions are funnelled and out of which all benefits are paid. The fund is usually kept segregated from the other assets of the sponsor. This method is usually required of private pension plans, although in practice some pension plans may be only partially funded. Because of the taxation powers of governments (including access to the money supply) governments are viewed as being financially secure and hence the risk element in the pay-as-you-go plan is eliminated, or at least significantly reduced.

Further features may be incorporated to cover employees who change employers. Portability provisions enable employees to carry their pension credits from one employer to another when changing jobs. This is the case with the Canada and Quebec Pension Plans. Portability can be provided through reciprocal agreements between employers. However, because private employer-sponsored plans can vary so much in structure, such reciprocity is difficult to achieve. This is where vesting becomes particularly important. Vesting refers to the right of employees changing jobs prior to retirement to all or part of their pension credits made by the employer on their behalf, whether those benefits are taken in cash or as a deferred pension. This provision removes the obligation of the employee to remain in a pension plan until retirement in order to qualify for pension benefits, since vesting establishes the benefits to which individuals are entitled if they change jobs. In Canada, if pensions are not vested, employees changing employers will usually get back only their own contributions to the plan plus the accumulated interest. Vesting is now usually associated with locking-in provisions that prevent employees from withdrawing their own, or their employer's, contribution in cash and require the acceptance of a deferred pension payable at the normal age of retirement.

PENSION HISTORY IN CANADA

The first pension legislation in Canada was the Superannuation Act of 1870, which made some pension provision for civil servants. Subsequently, the Pension Fund Societies Act of 1887 permitted federally incorporated companies to establish pension-funds societies. The Government Annuities Act of 1908 facilitated and encouraged individuals to save for their old age by permitting the government to sell annuities to the public at favourable rates. The first significant federal government intervention in the social welfare field occurred with the introduction of the Old Age Pension Act in 1927. This provided a framework for cost-sharing arrangements with the provinces to provide means-tested pensions to all needy individuals aged 70 years and over.

In 1951, with the introduction of the Old Age Security (OAS) Act, the federal government assumed full responsibility for the provision of a universal flat rate (as opposed to means-tested) old age pension at age 70, subject only to a residence requirement. This was funded by a special old age security tax. For the first time this guaranteed some income security for all older people. At the same time, the Old Age Assistance Act provided for federal contributions to means-tested pension programmes administered by the provinces for people aged between 65 and 69. Any additional retirement income was still expected to be provided through either personal saving or private pension plans.

In spite of these initiatives, there remained the problem that most employees suffered a substantial decline in income upon retirement, and none of the legislated schemes offered income replacement options. Institutionalized occupational pension plans and, to a lesser extent, registered retirement savings plans (RRSPs, introduced in 1957), experienced rapid growth over the

1950s and early 1960s, but inadequacies persisted. These concerns resulted in provincial initiatives, particularly in Quebec and Ontario, that culminated in 1965 in the Canada and Quebec Pension Plans (C/QPP). Combined, this was a compulsory and contributory plan designed to ensure a minimum rate of earnings replacement for those reaching the age of 65. Negotiation with the provinces resulted in the national plan on the condition that the investment funds were made available for provincial use, and these funds were secured by long-term (20-year) provincial government bonds.

This was combined with provincial legislation covering private pension plans in Ontario and, subsequently, in other provinces. Under this system, the universal OAS provided the income floor, available at age 65 by 1970, and a 1966 amendment provided a means-tested, guaranteed income supplement (GIS) in addition to OAS benefits for the very needy. The income replacement concerns were then handled through the C/QPP. In 1985 the benefit provisions were modified to permit a flexible retirement age between 55 and 75 with fewer years of contributions and hence lower benefits available at earlier ages, and vice versa. This system has provided the core of the publicly funded pension plans in Canada. Meanwhile, private pension plans and personal savings plans have also grown, especially in coverage if not in number. The income derived from these plans provides additional income for the retired employees in Canada.

One writer, sociologist John Myles, has estimated that payments under OAS, GIS and C/QPP account for approximately 60 per cent of the pension incomes of older Canadians. Payments from private or occupational pension plans account for a further 20 per cent, while personal assets (savings and financial investments) make up the remaining 20 per cent. However, the same author notes that these proportions vary with age, with the government proportion increasing with age as a result of reduced wages (if relevant), reduced savings and inflation erosion of both savings and private pensions.

Not surprisingly, therefore, poorer people depend on government contributions most, in which case they can account for around 70 per cent of income, especially for women. OAS payments are taxable, so the poor who pay no taxes get to retain all their benefits, while tax-paying pensioners will return in taxes some proportion of their OAS benefits. The GIS only goes to the poorest seniors and is non-taxable. Approximately 25 per cent of GIS beneficiaries receive the full amount; many more receive partial GIS payments. Single pensioners are more likely to qualify for the GIS because their incomes are lower. Since women generally live longer than men the majority of GIS recipients are women, and mostly widowed. Both OAS and GIS payments are indexed to the cost of living.

The Spouse's Allowance (SA) programme was added in 1975 to cover a low income pensioner's spouse who is aged 60 to 64. The benefits amount to the OAS plus the maximum GIS at the married rate. When the recipient reaches age 65, the SA payments cease and are replaced by the OAS/GIS pension. This programme is designed so that an eligible couple receives the same payments as a needy couple where both spouses are aged 65 and over. It has a survivor provision that permits SA payments even if the GIS pensioner dies. Not surprisingly, the vast majority (about 90 per cent) of SA beneficiaries are women.

The contributory C/QPP requires employee payments into the plan to be based on salary at a flat percentage rate (1.8 per cent in 1986) up to some maximum level ($444.60 in 1986). Employers are required to make matching payments. Self-employed persons make both contributions. Contributions are registered to the employee's credit so that when the employee retires, benefits are related to the accumulated contributions. However, as noted above, this is essentially a pay-as-you-go scheme. There are no accounts dedicated to individual employees, but there is vesting. There is portability, so that the pension entitlements move with the employees when they change employers. Moreover, benefits are indexed to inflation, are paid for the pensioner's remaining life and have survivor and disability provisions. The latter are particularly important to women who generally outlive their husbands and who, in the case of being unpaid homemakers, have no pensions of their own.

Currently, over 50 per cent of all people aged 65 and over are covered by the C/QPP. This can be expected to increase in the years ahead, as can the average level of payments, as more of the retiring Canadian labour force is covered by the plan. While this will increase government payments under the plan, it will also result in reduced GIS and SA payments in the future as fewer will qualify because of the increased coverage and level of C/QPP payments.

It has been estimated by the Conference Board of Canada that less than 50 per cent of Canadian employees are covered by private or occupational pension plans. Benefits under these plans account for only approximately 10 per cent of older Canadians' incomes. Consequently, most older people must rely on personal savings and investment income to assist with income replacement upon retirement. These sources account for approximately 30 per cent of older peoples' incomes. The government has encouraged more savings through Registered Retirement Savings Plans (RRSPs), which are tax-deferral financial instruments. Contributors pay tax only on the money actually withdrawn from the plan which, if in retirement, will be at a time when the person presumably has a lower income and hence a lower tax rate. The accumulated assets in RRSPs now exceed those in private pension plans in Canada.

There are also other sources of income or tax rebates for retirees. These include reduced property taxes for property owners and rent rebates for renters, old age income tax exemptions and sales tax rebates. Moreover, seniors are often eligible for other benefits such as reduced or subsidized medical, drug and home care service payment programmes, and a myriad of price reductions — in transportation fares, theatre tickets and so

on — in the semi-private and private sectors. These indirect subsidies could raise an older person's income by as much as 30 per
cent, although for most the figure is likely to be somewhat lower.

Unfortunately, as noted by many authors, this widespread
system of pension plans and other programmes available to
retirees does not *guarantee* a satisfactory income for older
Canadians in retirement for a variety of reasons. In spite of these
plans and programmes, many pensioners, particularly older
single women, still live in poverty. Even the combined income
security payments of the OAS, GIS and SA may be insufficient
for life in an expensive city, especially when the economies ac-
cruing to couples sharing expenses are no longer available upon
the death of a spouse.

In addition, the income replacement features available in the
C/QPP and private pension plans are unavailable to many
employees. People who retired prior to the introduction of the
C/QPP in 1966, or those who never worked in paid employment,
are not eligible. Workers in seasonal occupations or industries,
those who work part-time, or work for small businesses and have
low paying jobs are often not eligible for private pensions and
hence have no retirement income from this source. This often in-
tensifies the poverty cycle since the poor do not have access to
these types of pensions and become relatively poorer. And those
who do have this pension income may see it eroded by inflation
since few private pensions are automatically indexed to inflation. Add to this the uncertainty of corporate survivorship in a
rapidly changing world, and the lack of vesting and portability
in occupational pension plans, and it is apparent that such plans
cannot be relied upon in their current forms to provide a substantial and stable supplement to the pensioner's income.

PENSION REFORM

Much has been written on pension reform in Canada, especially
over the late 1970s and early 1980s. A 1982 Federal government

report entitled *Better Pensions for Canadians* was subsequently reviewed by a Parliamentary Task Force (the Firth Commission) but its recommendations are receiving attention very slowly. These recommendations covered the entire pension income system.

With respect to income security, the Task Force recommended increasing the OAS payments to bring them closer to the average industrial wage, and increasing GIS payments for single pensioners to approximately two-thirds of the benefits for couples, thus recognizing the increased expenses associated with living alone. In addition, it recommended extending the SA programme to include widows and widowers aged 60 to 64.

For income replacement through the C/QPP, the Task Force recommended increasing the maximum pensionable earnings so that individuals could contribute more, and receive more, when they retired. It recommended credit-splitting so that retirement benefits are divided between spouses in the event of the ineligibility of the remaining spouse, marriage breakdown, disability or death. A surviving spouse would then be eligible for 65 per cent of the couple's combined C/QPP benefits. Perhaps the most controversial of the recommendations was the homemaker's pension option. Under this option, couples who wish to avail themselves of this benefit would have to contribute more, although special subsidies were recommended for families with low incomes.

A wide variety of recommendations were made for income replacement through private pension plans, focusing primarily on portability and vesting. Portability was to be ensured through a new Registered Pension Account that would belong to the employee and be transferable with a change of employers. A locked-in provision was recommended. Inflation indexing, and full vesting for private pension funds after two years employment were also recommended. The Task Force also suggested changes to pension legislation and the Bankruptcy Act to prevent creditors from claiming pension funds as financial assets on which they have a claim in the case of bankruptcy. Finally, the Task Force addressed the specific problems women encounter by proposing eligibility after one year of service and for all part-time employees, credit-splitting in the event of marriage break-down and survivor benefits in the event of death, which would not be automatically withdrawn in the event of remarriage. While potentially far-reaching, these proposals would not benefit those employees who work for organizations with no private pension plans.

The Task Force's recommendations form the core of pension reform in almost all jurisdictions in Canada. Though their accep-tance is widespread, there remains considerable resistance to pension reform along these lines. The next section explores some of the reasons for this resistance.

PENSION REFORM RESISTANCE

Why has pension reform been slow in materializing? More specifically, why do the above recommendations remain largely unimplemented a number of years later?

Some changes are in progress. In 1985 changes were made in pension benefits for government and Crown Corporation employees. These included mandatory locked-in vesting after two years, improved portability through extended use of RRSPs, extensions to part-time employees with sufficient earnings (35 per cent of maximum pensionable earnings), survivor benefits at a rate of at least 60 per cent of the relevant couple rate and credit and payment splitting in the event of marriage breakdown.

However, most of the resistance to pension reform has centred on cost considerations. In an aging society the cost of pensions increases even without any "enrichments" to the programme. Obviously, enrichments, either through improved benefits for existing contributors or through extended coverage, will only exacerbate this problem. The private sector has claimed that it cannot afford to implement the changes proposed for the government programmes and remain "competitive." Even the CPP expects to increase the combined contribution rate by more than 100 per cent over the next 25 years (from 3.6 per cent in 1986 to 7.6 per cent in 2011) to keep the plan solvent. And even this is before the baby boomers start retiring. If the traditional retirement age of 65 is maintained, the first of the baby boomers born in 1947 will retire in 2012. For the following 20 years the baby-boom generation will be retiring, and placing substantial financial strain on the entire pension system.

To get an indication of these pressures, demographers have traditionally examined dependency ratios. The old-age dependency ratio is defined as the number of seniors for each person of working age. In essence, this is similar to expressing the expenditure (or beneficiary) base over the tax (or contributor) base, and hence is an indicator of the surplus or deficit in society (or in a plan). Thus, over time trends in this ratio indicate relative pressures. With the baby-boom generation all of working age by 1981, this ratio remains at historically low levels until around 2015 when it starts to move upward at a rapid rate.

While such ratios remain relevant to individual pension plans, they are not as relevant for society as a whole since it is conceivable that resource savings can be made elsewhere that will take some of the pressure off increasing expenditures. With a projected lower proportion of young people in Canadian society in the years ahead, this provides a logical focus for such savings. If it is assumed that such transfers are proportional to the numbers of people in the age groups concerned, they are not sufficient to prevent an increase in the dependency ratio for the Canadian society after 2011. By 2031 and thereafter, the dependency ratio stabilizes at around 1.7 potential taxpayers for each dependent, considerably lower than the current 2.1 and the maximum 2.25 in 2011. However, it is above the figure of 1.4 experienced at the height of the baby boom in 1961.

Even these figures are somewhat misleading. It has been shown that in terms of current government expenditures it costs between two and three times more to support a senior on all government programmes than a younger person. Given this fact, it has been calculated that pressures on society will increase between 2 and 9 per cent by 2011. Over the following decade the projected increase is between 22 and 26 per cent and a further 23 to 29 per cent over the subsequent decade.

These are potentially alarming numbers. They are based on continuation of current trends with respect to expenditure financing, and assume that revenues are proportional to the number of workers. This is unlikely in a world of improved productivity, so the actual pressures are likely to be ameliorated by productivity growth. The more rapid the growth, the less serious the situation will be. Nonetheless, these calculations are symbolic of the current resistance to extensive pension reform.

In a nonfunded pay-as-you-go plan, the fundamental issue comes down to income redistribution — not only from the young to the elderly, but also from the working aged to the elderly. Whether it will take place easily or with considerable strain has a lot to do with Canada's economic performance in the years ahead. Nonetheless, older people — unlike the young — can exercise their vote at the ballot box and, with ever increasing numbers, their votes will carry greater political power. It is likely that this power will be used to secure economic benefits, or, at the very least, to make sure that existing benefits are not eroded. The severity of the situation will not be apparent until the second decade of the twenty-first century, but careful decisions in the years ahead with respect to education, health care and so on are essential if the problem is to be made easier to handle than it appears from today's vantage point.

4

EDUCATION

Education is often considered to be the domain of the young. Indeed in Canada, as in many countries, education is legally compulsory up to a certain age — currently fifteen years in most provinces. Traditionally, education is concentrated in the early years of an individual's life, with elementary school being immediately followed by secondary (or high) school and, for those who qualify, the choice thereafter from a variety of post-secondary options. Sometimes a student may take a break from schooling — for example, between the secondary and post-secondary streams, or within the post-secondary stream such as between a Bachelors and a higher degree — but for most students their education is generally completed in approximately the first one-third of their lifetime or earlier. It can be argued that this is a wise decision from both the individual's and society's viewpoint since it leaves the remainder of the lifetime to reap the returns from this initial "investment." Aging, however, is beginning to leave its mark on this traditional approach, especially in the post-secondary system. Not only is the massive baby-boom generation now entirely of post-secondary age, leading to increased numbers in these instituations, but many are now pursuing their education in different directions from their initial interests and to higher levels. Moreover, many are returning to these institutions after significant absences, often for professional reasons — upgrading or retraining — but also for personal reasons. Broadly speaking, this means that, in spite of institutional constraints on individual choices, education is becoming increasingly relevant to members of the over-40 society.

Education for formal credit in Canada is delivered at three main levels. While there is some regional diversity, the elementary level generally covers grades one to six, the secondary level generally covers grades seven to twelve or thirteen, and the post-secondary level includes both university and community colleges. Within each level there are both full-time and part-time students, with the definition of the latter varying by jurisdiction, although usually a part-time student is defined as a registered student who is not taking a full course load.

In addition to these formal programmes there are a multitude of non-credit courses and programmes at all educational levels often offered under the description of continuing education. These cover both vocational and avocational (for example, hobby-related) subjects and are usually offered on a fee basis. In this setting, course offerings are often conditional on enrollment levels and prerequisite requirements, if they exist, are kept to a minimum.

Of course, educational offerings are by no means limited to educational institutions. Many organizations provide instructional courses outside the recognized schools, colleges and universities. Some of these are offered by professional associations and other employee groups. Some are offered on a fee basis in the private sector to respond to specific needs either not provided, or not provided adequately, by the educational institutions. Some are provided by non-profit organizations, or by community groups, to provide information and services on a variety of topics. In addition, there are the traditional media outlets — television, radio and the press — which have always served as an educational source of one form or another. The potential list of providers of educational services is almost endless, as are the services provided.

This chapter is limited to the roles performed by the traditional educational institutions — elementary and secondary schools and, especially, post-secondary institutions — in meeting the needs of an aging society. This is not intended to minimize the importance of the various other educational providers to the over-40 society, but rather to focus on the challenges awaiting the formal educational institutions as a result of an aging population. Since it will be argued that these challenges are imminent and substantial, a full understanding of educational issues will not only provide a guide to government policy in this area, but will also provide a guide to the trends likely to affect the providers of all educational services in Canada in the years ahead.

ENROLLMENT PATTERNS

The most complete and, in this context, useful enrollment data are compiled for Canadian universities. The summary of the data in Table 4.1 includes full-time and part-time enrollments, and undergraduate and graduate enrollments. It excludes non-credit (continuing education) enrollments. For the purposes of this analysis, enrollments have been divided into three age groups: under 25, 25 to 40 and over 40. While the latter are the main focus of this book, the 25 to 40 age group also comprises the enrollment potential of the over-40 age group over the remainder of the twentieth century. They are, therefore, particularly relevant to educational policy over the 1990s and beyond, and are identified separately to provide an indication of future trends.

Canada's university student population is clearly aging. Of the slightly more than 520,000 students in 1976, almost two in five — actually 37.2 per cent — were aged 25 and over. A decade later the student population comprised almost 758,000 students and the proportion of students aged 25 and over had risen to 43.9 per cent. This means that by the middle of the 1980s almost nine in every twenty university students in Canada were aged 25 and over.

TABLE 4.1

University Enrollment Totals by Type and Age, Canada, 1976-86

Type/Age	Numbers			%		
	1976	1981	1986	1976	1981	1986
Total:						
Under 25	327,272	371,990	425,129	62.8	57.3	56.1
25-40	166,021	233,055	273,093	31.9	35.9	36.0
Over 40	27,900	43,872	59,367	5.4	6.8	7.8
Total Under-graduate:						
Under 25	314,471	357,971	410,795	68.0	62.8	61.6
25-40	124,539	175,157	206,341	26.9	30.7	31.0
Over 40	23,271	36,976	49,277	5.0	6.5	7.4
Total Graduate:						
Under 25	12,801	14,019	14,334	21.7	17.8	15.7
25-40	41,482	57,898	66,752	70.4	73.5	73.2
Over 40	4,629	6,896	10,090	7.9	8.7	11.1
Total Full-time:						
Under 25	288,920	316,962	361,830	81.2	79.3	76.6
25-40	62,872	77,929	102,772	17.7	19.5	21.8
Over 40	3,913	4,990	7,661	1.1	1.2	1.6
Total Part-time:						
Under 25	38,352	55,028	63,299	23.2	22.1	22.2
25-40	103,149	155,126	170,321	62.3	62.3	59.7
Over 40	23,987	38,882	51,706	14.5	15.6	18.1

Source: Statistics Canada, Post-seconday Education Section, and calculations by the authors.

The proportion of the over-40 age group has also been increasing from 5.4 per cent in 1976 to 7.8 per cent a decade later. In the middle of the 1980s nearly 60,000 university students in Canada were in this age bracket. While total university enrollment in Canada grew by an average of 3.8 per cent annually over this period, the fastest growing age group was the oldest, over-40 group. Annual enrollment growth in this group averaged 7.8 per cent over the decade, compared with 5.1 per cent for the middle 25 to 40 age group and only 2.7 per cent for the youngest group, those under 25. These comparative growth rates underscore the aging of Canada's university student population.

Where are these older students in the universities? In the undergraduate student body the dominant age groups are the younger ages. While this will not come as a surprise, it is notable that 38.4 per cent — almost two in five undergraduate students — are aged 25 and over. This is an increase from 32 per cent — or fewer than one in three students — a decade earlier. Not surprisingly, the graduate student population is noticeably older. By 1986, 84.3 per cent of graduate students were aged 25 and over, and this represented an increase of six percentage points over the previous decade. Within this group, over 11 per cent — at least one in ten graduate students — are over 40. This proportion also increased over the decade.

Turning to the alternative division into full-time and part-time enrollments, it is apparent that part-time students are older. Although approximately three out of four full-time students are from the under-25 age group, the proportion has been decreasing over the decade. Moreover, during the same period, the number of full-time students aged over 40 almost doubled. By 1986 there were over 7,650 full-time students in Canadian universities over the age of 40. If this figure appears surprisingly high, it pales by comparison to the number of part-time university students of this age. Enrollment in this group has increased from almost 24,000 students in 1976 to 51,700 in 1986, an increase of 115 per cent, or an average annual growth of 8 per cent over the decade. By the middle of the 1980s they comprised over 18 per cent of part-time enrollments. In addition, the 25 to 40 age group accounted for a further 60 per cent. This means that only 22 per cent of part-time university students — or approximately one in five — were aged under 25.

TABLE 4.2

University Enrollment Details by Type and Age, Canada, 1976-86

Type/Age	Numbers			%		
	1976	1981	1986	1976	1981	1986
Under-graduate Full-time:						
Under 25	278,072	305,275	349,739	87.4	86.5	84.0
25-40	37,948	45,182	62,489	11.9	12.8	15.0
Over 40	2,244	2,617	4,162	0.7	0.7	1.0
Under-graduate Part-time:						
Under 25	36,399	52,696	61,056	25.3	24.3	24.4
25-40	86,591	129,975	143,852	60.1	59.9	57.5
Over 40	21,027	34,359	45,115	14.6	15.8	18.0
Graduate Full-time:						
Under 25	10,848	11,687	12,091	29.0	25.0	21.6
25-40	24,924	32,747	40,283	66.6	70.0	72.1
Over 40	1,669	2,373	3,499	4.1	5.1	6.3
Graduate Part-time:						
Under 25	1,953	2,332	2,243	9.1	7.3	6.3
25-40	16,558	25,151	26,469	77.1	78.6	75.0
Over 40	2,960	4,523	6,591	13.8	14.1	18.7

Source: Statistics Canada, Post-secondary Education Section, and calculations by the authors.

These findings are further supported by the detailed data presented in Table 4.2. These data show that even the traditional university base — the full-time undergraduate student population — is aging. Those aged under 25 have gradually fallen from 87.4 per cent of this group in 1976 to 84 per cent a decade later. While it is clear that this group is dominated by the younger student, it will come as a surprise to many that 16 per cent of full-time undergraduates are now aged 25 and over. And those aged over 40 in this population now number over 4,000 students, an 85 per cent increase over the previous decade. Three out of four part-time undergraduate enrollments are aged 25 and over. Although there has been little change in this proportion over the decade, older students represent an increasing proportion of this group. By 1986, 18 per cent of part-time undergraduates are aged 40 years and over, up from 14.6 per cent a decade earlier. The proportion of full-time graduate students aged 25 and over increased from 71 per cent in 1976 to 78.4 per cent by 1986 and, once again, the share of the over-40 group increased over the decade. By 1986 there were 3,500 full-time students aged over 40 in Canadian graduate programmes. By far the oldest university student population is that of the part-time graduate students where three out of four are aged 25 to 40, and almost one out of five are aged over 40. This student population has also been aging, with the share of those aged under 25 falling from 9.1 per cent in 1976 to 6.3 per cent in 1986.

As evidence of these trends, the "extension" Woodsworth College at the University of Toronto has the largest student population of all the University colleges. The vast majority of its approximately 7,500 students are part-time. Currently they range in age from 21 to 96 and approximately two-thirds are women. Undergraduate courses are free to senior citizens and a seniors group of over 200 comprises one of the most active groups in the college community. Woodsworth College has improved accessibility to university education by offering courses in off-campus locations. This has attracted students from the community, offices and assembly-line shifts among others, and invariably these are older students.

University enrollment trends show clearly that:

- there has been a significant aging of the university student population in Canada over the past decade;

- university graduate programmes, not surprisingly, attract older students;
- older students are more likely to be registered as part-time rather than as full-time students; and
- the over-40 group is the fastest growing age group in the university student population.

TABLE 4.3

Full-time Community College Enrollments by Age, Canada, 1976-1986

Type/Age	Number			%		
	1976[1]	1981[2]	1986	1976[1]	1981[2]	1986
Under 25	81,495	151,994	275,052	88.0	90.6	85.5
25-40	9,587	14,204	40,058	10.3	8.5	12.5
Over 40	1,564	1,575	6,611	1.7	0.9	2.1

[1] Excludes the provinces of Quebec, Prince Edward Island and Saskatchewan.
[2] Excludes continuing students in Quebec.
Source: Statistics Canada, Post-secondary Education Section.

The data for university enrollments likely mirrors a general enrollment trend throughout the educational system. Data for other parts of the educational system are severely limited in many respects, especially with respect to their consistency over time. For example, Table 4.3 summarizes full-time community college enrollments in Canada over the same period using the same age breakdowns as the previous table. These data show the same trends noted above. Even for full-time enrollments at the community college level (where there are no graduate programmes) the share of the under-25 age group has been declining from 88 per cent in 1976 to 85.5 per cent by 1986. Moreover, in 1986

TABLE 4.4

Elementary and Secondary Enrollments by Age,
Ontario, 1976-1986[1]

	Number			%		
	1976	1981	1986	1976	1981	1986
Elementary:[2]						
Under 20	2,037,833	1,869,035	1,836,826	99.7	99.3	98.6
20 & Over	5,251	13,502	26,146	0.3	0.7	1.4
Secondary:						
Under 20	608,207	557,004	592,714	99.2	98.0	96.2
20 & Over	4,848	11,631	23,711	0.8	2.0	3.8

[1] Publicly funded enrollments for Roman Catholic schools included in secondary data in 1986.
[2] Public plus private enrollments.
Source: Ontario Ministry of Education.

there were over 6,600 full-time students aged over 40 in Canadian community colleges. Undoubtedly the number and the share of older students under part-time registration and sponsored courses would be significantly higher, but unfortunately these data are not collected on a general basis.

Fragmentary data at other levels of the educational system lend support to these trends. For example, in Ontario (Table 4.4) the proportions of older students in elementary and secondary schools have been increasing. In total in 1986 there were almost 50,000 students aged 20 years and over in elementary and secondary schools in the province, a figure that represented a five-fold increase over the previous decade. Just how many of these are aged over 40 years is not known, but the trends are likely to be comparable to those for post-secondary enrollments.

Similar conclusions are likely to be applicable to non-credit continuing education enrollments, and enrollments in other less formal educational settings. In essence the trend towards the older student is now widespread and well established. This trend mirrors the comparable trend in the population at large, and the future for the educational system can be expected to largely follow the projections in the population outlined in Chapter 1. This suggests some important policy issues facing educational institutions in the years ahead.

EDUCATION AND THE OLDER STUDENT

Why do older students continue in, or re-enter, the educational system? There are probably two main reasons for this decision: to train or retrain for a career, or to pursue an avocation. Of course, these two reasons need not be mutually exclusive. For some their vocation may also be their avocation, such as the professional astronomer or diver, whereas for others their avocation may evolve into their vocation, such as the antique collector who becomes an antique dealer. It is much more likely that the former necessitates enrollment for credit, often towards a degree or diploma, the receipt of which then facilitates a career movement. In this sense, education is viewed largely as an investment, with up-front costs (fees, books, time and so on) in return for anticipated future benefits (career advancement). The latter type of education is much less likely to require enrollment for credit. Education in this sense is viewed largely as consumption, to be enjoyed today with no direct expectations of future benefits. The costs are usually lower and the benefits immediate — any future benefits in terms of individual career advancement or some form of contribution to society, are usually viewed as "bonuses."

Whatever the motivation for the appearance of older students in traditional educational institutions, their presence raises a plethora of administrative and evaluative concerns. For example, it is usual for admission criteria to depend on evidence of previous satisfactory performance in the educational system, often to a prescribed level. The criteria may be relaxed for "mature" students, but often some evidence of previous educational exposure is necessary. The older the student, the more out-of-date this educational experience is likely to be and the more difficult it becomes to evaluate the individual in terms of background or preparation for the proposed programme of study. Even apparently mundane requests like filing a copy of a course reading list with the application may be impossible to satisfy if the student has misplaced it and the professor is no longer available or does not keep detailed back files. And if it is available, the evaluation of the current relevance of the past course content is likely to be difficult at best. It is likely to become a contentious issue if the older student seeks some course credit for academic work previously completed, either to save on tuition fees or, more likely, to speed up the programme of studies. Such issues are likely to be intensified if enrollment in the programme is limited, so that the admission of one student necessitates the omission of some other student. In this environment the student with the better documented application, which almost invariably favours the younger student, is likely to be granted admission over the older student. All of these considerations may well be conveniently packaged under the rubric of "maintaining academic quality." It is almost inevitable that a course taken twenty years earlier will be considered as effectively irrelevant for educational preparation to a current course, whereas one taken the previous year would be judged as "required preparation."

The Achilles Heel in this approach is the appropriate evaluation of labour market experience. If an educational institution ignores the value of education on the job the older student is penalized. Yet, it is admittedly difficult to arrive at an objective evaluation of on-the-job experience or training, especially as it pertains to a particular academic programme or course. While this fact is currently recognized within educational institutions, there remains a concern in the older student population that insufficient weight is given to this experience in such things as admittance and decisions on advanced standing.

The scheduling of courses may also impose burdens on the older student, especially if education is being pursued in conjunction with ongoing family or employment obligations. To address this problem, educational institutions sometimes offer one or more sections of multisectional courses in evening hours. As well, continuing and adult education departments have experimented with early morning and off-campus course offerings with some apparent success. However, there is still little respite for the on-campus single-section, usually upper-level university courses, where the student must readjust his or her schedule to fit into the traditional full-time student routine. And it becomes even more acute at the graduate level where, ironically, there are even more older students.

Moreover, the residency requirements for diplomas and degrees almost always require the student's physical presence at the educational institution for some prolonged period of time. The opportunity to do part-time and correspondence graduate studies in Canada is almost unknown. This is likely a totally untapped source of educational demand, particularly in an aging population. Without these flexibilities the observed growth in enrollments of older students is even more remarkable, since they are entering a system that is not particularly adapted to their needs.

In addition, even after these "hurdles" have been cleared and the older student has entered, there remain concerns with the appropriate teaching and evaluation of the student. It is widely acknowledged that teaching and evaluation schemes that emphasize memory tend to be biased against the older student. This means that older students may not perform as well in courses characterized by the traditional end-of-year, closed-book examination format. The opportunity to have more frequent

examinations where less memory is required is likely to be helpful to the older student, as is the introduction of term work, such
as papers, in which the older students can demonstrate the
relevance of their work experience. Marks for class participation
may also benefit the older student since age tends to make the
individual more mature and confident (although not always in
the educational setting). Also, it is hard not to believe that certain methods of teaching are more effective for older students.
Certainly the use of illustrations that draw on "real-world" situations are likely to be more widely accepted and received by those
who can relate to them. Perhaps the use of handouts to be studied
outside the classroom, combined with some classroom time
taken up with discussion, is more beneficial for older students
than the more traditional uni-directional instruction approach.
Methods of teaching and evaluation can be just as important as
the other dimensions of the educational milieu for the success of
older students in the educational system.

The growing numbers of older students in the educational
system raises many challenges. Some of these have been recognized, but most are beyond those currently confronted in today's
educational institutions. Under these conditions individual
choices are likely being constrained, which makes all the more
remarkable the rapid growth in the older student population.
With an educational system more adapted to the needs of the
older student it could have undoubtedly been even faster.

EDUCATION AND THE LABOUR MARKET

The challenges posed by the labour market as a result of the
population aging have been reviewed in Chapter 2. It is important to see the connections between these labour market challenges and the educational system. The investment nature of
education has always been recognized as an essential benefit of
the educational system from a social viewpoint. In this system
students are provided with an array of skills that will serve them

well in the labour market, and enable them to become "productive" members of society. It is for this reason that formal education is often provided in the public sector since it provides skills from which both the individual and society benefit. At the lower educational levels, general skills like reading, writing and arithmetic are provided. As the individual proceeds to higher educational levels these skills are enhanced and, often, more specific skills provided. These may be abstract, or applied, or both. Different parts of the educational system specialize in different aspects of this training, with universities generally associated with the more abstract training and community colleges generally associated with the more applied training. Of course, there are apparent exceptions such as the professional faculties in universities (for example, business, law, medicine, nursing and agriculture). Once again the division is not clear-cut.

Nonetheless, there is one common thread linking all of these activities and that is the provision of skills that can be utilized, in one way or another, in the labour market. This is the essential link between educational organizations and the labour market.

Population aging affects both. The reflection of population aging on educational enrollments has been reviewed earlier in this chapter. But the link is even more interdependent. Population aging by itself could well lead to fewer students in a world where education is acquired early in life and then "used up" over the individual's working life. In the context of a baby-boom generation now in their 20s and 30s, this might explain some of the increase in graduate enrollments over the last decade as this generation completes its educational training, but it would also imply a reduced educational demand at lower educational levels and in the future as most would have already acquired their requisite education. In this hypothetical world there would be no need for older students to return for more education, except insofar as their education had been interrupted at an earlier stage (perhaps by a war or family catastrophe).

The interdependent relationship between aging and enrollments arises in a world where education is a continuous process throughout an individual's life. This may be the result of rapid depreciation of received skills because of technological advancements in either capital (machines) or labour (management). In such a world it is necessary to "invest" in maintaining existing skills, or developing new skills more appropriate to the ever changing labour market. This view of education helps to explain why older students appear in the educational system and why, often, they do not always take courses at more advanced levels or towards new degrees or diplomas. It may also explain the more rapid growth in the enrollment of older students in recent times since, if the speed of technological change picks up (as might be argued has occurred with the introduction of such technological developments as the micro-chip and computers), the human capital skills depreciate more rapidly, thus necessitating even more "investment" in skill maintenance and retraining. This could explain some of the increase in the number of older students over the last decade.

It is likely that this type of education will occur at the upper educational levels since technological change tends to be at the frontiers of the work environment rather than at the basic levels. Yet, its ultimate percolation down to the basic levels will mean that no employee is insulated from the need for educational retraining.

The interdependence goes even further in a society characterized by a large baby-boom generation that, because of its size, generates limited promotional possibilities over a person's life. As outlined in some detail in Chapter 2, it will probably be necessary in the future for the baby boomers to combine lateral moves with promotional moves throughout their careers. Since lateral moves almost inevitably involve some change in occupation there is likely to be a continuing demand for education at most levels of the educational system to facilitate these lateral moves. The director of marketing may have to learn the fundamentals

and skills of human resource planning to become the new director of human resources, while the old director of human resources will find it necessary to take some courses in marketing in
order to assume the colleague's old position. As a result of the
"swap" both will be confronted with new challenges and opportunities. And the educational system can play an essential role in
both fostering and facilitating these moves. However, educators
must not only recognize the opportunity; they must also address
the special needs of older students. Courses for these students
may have to be modular and intense, rather than spread out over
the standard academic year; they may have to be offered off-campus and on the site of the student's employer; and they may have
to involve instruction and evaluation methods that are innovative and different from current practices.

If the educational system does not respond to these emerging
needs, both students and their employers are likely to seek alternatives. These involve the creating of employer in-house training programmes, or turning to non-Canadian suppliers of on-site
modular courses. With declining growth in the labour force it
will be in the employer's interest to encourage and fund these
courses, in total or in part, because it will be one of the few ways
left to introduce flexibility into their aging work force.

The opportunities for traditional educational institutions to
play an even more direct role in educating at all levels for the
labour market have never been greater. Whether these institutions can meet the challenge remains to be seen.

EDUCATION FOR LEISURE

The pursuit of knowledge for self-gratification is the second
reason older students return to the educational system. In this
context, one of the key indicators of demand is the current
amount of education people have. The more educated people are,
the more likely they are to seek further education to satisfy their
personal goals. While this is somewhat less true in the more

general community-based educational endeavours, it is particularly true in the formal educational system. And since the level of education has risen noticeably in Canada, especially in the baby-boom generation, it is likely that this will provide an ongoing source of educational demand in the future.

There is already ample evidence for this trend. Many colleges and universities have developed programmes for their senior alumni. Glendon College, in Toronto, has its Third Age Learning Associates, while the provincial government's New Horizon Grants have facilitated the establishment of the Living and Learning Programme at the University of Toronto. Another, apparently very successful venture, is Elderhostel where groups of seniors travel to universities of their choice in the summer months and enroll in special courses tailored to their particular interests. This also has the advantage of utilizing university facilities (and, perhaps, faculty) at a time when they are not normally used to capacity.

Of course, such enrollments are not necessarily limited to the senior population. All ages of the population are potential candidates for this type of educational experience and, ultimately, this will need to be recognized by educators. From the institution's perspective, offering avocational courses is a potentially high profile method for maintaining alumni identification with their alma mater — and, of course, such identification is an essential element in gift-giving and bequest donations. When viewed in this light, the economics of such course offerings may appear quite favourable, even at present rates. It is important to recognize, however, that education of this kind is primarily for consumption and will be purchased in similar fashion as other "goods." Since no personal financial return is expected from avocational courses, as is the case for investment-type education, the fee structure will probably need to be below that of the investment-type education courses.

CONCLUSION

In an interview Dr. Northrop Frye noted:

One welcome change that has occurred over the last few years is that the university is no longer a monopoly of the 18 to 22-year-old age group. It makes a big difference when you realize that there are some people in the class old enough to be the parents of others, that you are not just talking to young people. The tensions in the class become very exciting and, of course, the generation gap gets closed up on all sides...the salvation of the university lies in making it a place for adults at various stages to come for retraining in skills which have now become out of date, or for a renewed contact with things that have become hazy in their minds. I think the university will never do its job in society until a great mass of people of all ages feel they can come and get their lives revitalized. The process is somewhat like a religious retreat, except that it would be a much more permanent thing because being involved in some form of cultural activity is what really makes one a human being.

Education is likely to continue to play an important role in our aging society. Student enrollments are already becoming older and the future holds even more importance for older students. They will be furthering their education for professional and personal reasons. Rapid technological change and blocked career paths for the baby boomers will intensify the need for education for the labour market, while a better educated populace, and increasing numbers in the senior age groups, will support the need for leisure-type education. Whether these courses will be offered in the traditional or formal educational environment remains an open question. It requires the recognition and resolution of a variety of issues and problems unique to the older student. If these opportunities are not seized by the traditional educational institutions in the years ahead, they will likely be provided for by a variety of non-traditional sources in the public and private sectors.

5

HEALTH CARE

Health is one of the primary concerns for an aging population. This is true for the individual, but as the number of older and very old Canadians continues to grow, the increasing costs of health care creates great anxiety for society as a whole, and seems to be threatening the universal health-care system.

In this respect, two points need to be made at the outset. First, an aging population is not the only cause of rising health-care costs. Other factors, notably rapid advances in technology, and ever-increasing costs of goods and services, also contribute. Second, while alarmist predictions of catastrophe appear premature, some warning signals are flashing and appropriate changes in the health-care delivery system must be made. This involves both the individual, who must become involved in promoting his or her own health, and society, which must adopt a stance of health-promotion and disease-prevention. In short, our society must move from a health system that emphasizes diagnosis and treatment or "cure" to a multifaceted system that encompasses a broad understanding of all the factors contributing to physical and mental well-being. This shifts the focus from a highly medicalized approach, to one that is more socially oriented. Most Canadians, including health- and social-service professionals, endorse the broadly based World Health Organization definition of health as a "state of complete physical, mental and social well-being, and not merely the absence of disease or infirmity." It is known, for instance, that income level, social class, education, work, general physical and social environment, biological and genetic heritage all play a part in influencing the ability to maintain a state of good health.

FACTORS AFFECTING HEALTH

Income
It is widely acknowledged that the single most consistent relationship to health status is socio-economic level. A man earning a low income enters "old age" (defined by health status and life expectancy) around age 50, whereas a man earning a high income reaches the same stage around age 60. There is less of a difference for women, with low-income women entering "old age" at 60 and high-income women at 65. Poor men can expect to have four fewer years of disability-free life than wealthy men. In general, life expectancy for men of the highest income level is approximately 6 years greater than that for men at the lowest income level. For women, the difference is only about three years.

Canadians have one of the best health-care systems in the world, providing universal medical and hospital care. However, this universal health-care system, while improving the availability of services for all, does not obliterate the high correlation between income and health.

Environment
Environment, of course, is influenced to a considerable degree by income, since this affects available housing and transportation choices — two important factors in well-being. However, clean air and fresh, uncontaminated water clearly contribute to good health, and the quality of the work place contributes to reduced stress. The social environment, furthermore, is an important factor that is often overlooked. Attitudes and values will often determine how efficiently one can access information, or make contacts with social support groups. The latter ability seems to be critical as a close connection exists between the

presence of strong social support networks and individual well-being.

Life-style

Life-style is how you conduct your daily activities, and the choices you make in relation to these activities. To a significant extent, income and environmental factors influence life-style, but personal choice does play an important part. The important point is whether the chosen life-style uses or abuses the body and its potential.

Physical Activity

Physical activity is very important in achieving and maintaining good health. Unfortunately, many people tend to develop sedentary life-styles. Canada's adult population can be classified as 27 per cent active, 44 per cent moderately active and 29 per cent sedentary. Men tend to be more active than women. Many people are "turned off" by physical education in elementary school, where it quickly becomes competitive and stressful rather than "fun," and this resistance is carried through life. The baby boomers, or at least those who are well-educated and financially able, appear to be a notable exception. They are the mainstay of the burgeoning fitness industry. The problem is how to spread this newly acquired enthusiasm throughout the entire population, so that it includes both young children and older adults, as well as those with different ethnic and economic backgrounds. However, increasing emphasis on fitness among the young may result in a fitter older age group and the postponement of disability.

Nutrition

Nutrition has been a much neglected aspect of life-style, but it is becoming more and more accepted that, "we are what we eat." Over their lifetime women, particularly young girls, should be eating foods rich in calcium, and men and women should be eating fewer foods high in animal fat. Everyone should be eating less salt, less refined sugar and more fibre. There is, unfortunately, little emphasis on nutrition among health-care professionals, and physicians are often poorly informed and do not refer patients to nutritionists.

Substance Use and Abuse

This is another aspect of life-style that involves individual behaviour and choice. Since smoking is a habit that is extremely detrimental to one's health, it is a hopeful sign that society is moving in the direction of turning the work place, and public areas, into smoke-free environments. However, because nicotine is addictive, it is very difficult for some people to stop smoking. More men seem to have stopped smoking than women.

The use of alcohol in our society is also widespread, and alcoholism is an important health issue. Many lifelong abusers of alcohol do not survive into old age. Those who do are often significantly impaired. There is evidence that some people are drinking more as they retire. Since tolerance diminishes with increasing age, even moderate increases in drinking may lead to falls and other health problems. More older women are using alcohol to excess. It is frequently an unidentified problem, particularly in women.

The use of illicit drugs is equally a hazard to health and well-being. A wide range of drugs including marijuana, hashish, cocaine and heroin are used with varying degrees of prevalence, but the use of some drugs such as cocaine seems to be on the increase. These drugs are not used to any significant degree by the present elderly, but could cause problems for present users as they age.

Sexuality has a relationship to life-style and in recent years, with the awareness of the devastating effects of acquired immunodeficiency syndrome (AIDS), there is increased concern over life-styles that contribute to the spread of sexually communicated diseases.

All of the above life-style factors may require some form of consciousness-raising strategy — making people want to change their behaviour because there is some "payoff" for them in the short or long term. It is not easy to change long-established patterns of behaviour that are also influenced by social class, culture and ethnic background; however, all these factors influence our health and consequently are important issues in affecting the future of our health-care system.

The Aging Process

With advancing age, particularly very advanced age, there is an increased probability of developing acute and chronic health problems. Although most older adults consider themselves to be in good to excellent health, they utilize the health-care system more than other age groups. In fact, the probability of the development of a medical problem increases by the fiftieth year. Eighty-five per cent of the group 65 and over have some chronic condition, with fifty percent of these reporting that the problem has curtailed their activity to some extent. Only a small proportion, however, has trouble carrying out daily tasks until very old age (85 and over). There are important gender differences in that, although women have a longer average life expectancy they have more chronic conditions. The so-called "gender gap" in life expectancy is not fully understood, but is thought to be the result of a combination of genetic and life-style differences. There is some suggestion that the gap is closing. Men are showing a decline in death rate from heart disease and cancer particularly because they are smoking and drinking less, while women seem to be showing the effects of continued smoking, and what is considered increased stress due to multiple roles of worker and homemaker.

Changes in vision and hearing occur with advancing age. You only need to be in your forties to notice how much more difficult it is to read the telephone directory, or that your arm is not quite long enough to read the menu, especially in a dimly lit restaurant! Chronic conditions such as cardiovascular disease, hypertension, diabetes and musculo-skeletal changes resulting in arthritis and osteoporosis are all more frequent in the older age groups. These changes, however, begin to form in the middle-40s.

One of the most significant problems for the very old is the approximately 20 per cent of those over age 85 with senile dementia. The majority of these people suffer from senile dementia of the Alzheimer-type, and some from varying degrees of senile dementia due to cardiovascular changes that result in small strokes or major cerebro-vascular accidents. Although only approximately 5 per cent of those 65 and over suffer severe cognitive impairment, this incidence increases rapidly in the 85 and over group. This type of illness has implications for informal-care providers as well as the formal-care system. The stress of caring for impaired family members can take its toll on the care-giver's health. Women are the usual care-givers, either as spouses or daughters, and daughters-in-law. Men sometimes provide care for their wives but women are more likely to be institutionalized because of their tendency to outlive their spouses. Senile dementia is also reported to be slightly more frequent in women.

A major challenge for investigators of the aging process is to unravel the inevitable changes that occur in the human being even under optimal conditions. The next step will be to learn how to prevent certain conditions and how to promote better physical and mental health. The future may hold discoveries that will postpone or eliminate the negative, disabling features of aging.

THE HEALTH-CARE DELIVERY SYSTEM FOR AN AGING POPULATION

Canadians appear to support, almost as a political "sacred cow," the universal medical and hospital insurance system that is in place. Although the system varies somewhat from province to province, the basic principle of universal accessibility to good health care tends to be similar. While rising costs, resulting from inflation and the increasing use of expensive new technology, put a strain on our health-care system, the shift in the age structure of the population imposes a particular challenge. This is related to the higher proportionate use of medical and hospital resources by the older segment of the population, and also to the increased probability of need for long-term care, whether it be community or institutionally-based. Interestingly enough, there have been studies that indicate a very small percentage (approximately 8 per cent) of the elderly account for the highest use of health services.

The formal-care system involves care in hospitals, long-term institutions or at home, delivered by health- and social-service professionals. The system has been, and still is, primarily institutionally-based with the physician, particularly the family physician, as the primary entry point to the health system. This is a very costly health system, although Canada has contained health-care costs to about 9 per cent of the gross national product (GNP), while others such as the United States have seen their costs mounting to about 12 per cent of the GNP. However, it has been argued that Canada may have managed to keep costs down by not funding new technology research, and not implementing costly programmes and treatment techniques as quickly as elsewhere.

We are now capable of using high technology to prolong the life of the elderly, and of doing other costly procedures such as coronary bypass surgery, organ transplants and hip replacements, to name a few. But, as the health-care system comes under more pressure, important questions will arise. Who will receive expensive treatment? How do we distribute limited resources among the new technologies? To what extent should we prolong life, and who will make the decisions? These are all difficult questions and involve us as a society in profound moral and ethical dilemmas.

Social change is giving rise to other questions to which we have, as yet, no final answers. For example, we have some evidence that later-life pregnancies carry greater risk, yet we are seeing a significant proportion of the baby boomers postponing pregnancies until the middle to late 30s and early 40s. Delayed childbearing is associated with an increase in medical costs: the possibility of infertility increases with age, and infertility investigation and treatment involve a greater use of technology and tend to be very expensive. Expensive diagnostic procedures such as ultrasound are more likely to be used in these later pregnancies. Can the system afford to bear these costs? There is evidence, too, of stress on women who wish to carry out the multiple roles of worker, wife and mother. What resources should be put to use to reduce this stress? We know also that the increasing divorce rate has changed the way our children are cared for, but the effects of being brought up by a single parent, in shared custody, or of various arrangements of divided and multiple families are, as yet, unknown. Will this result in increased or reduced pressures on the health-care system? Research into the long-term effects of day care, and various models of day care, is as yet very limited.

One thing is clear: if we continue to deliver health care that places a heavy emphasis on cure and institutionalization, the costs will become unbearable. Canada today has the highest proportion of its elderly institutionalized than any other western industrialized country (see Table 5.1).

Surveys have indicated that 15 to 20 per cent or more of those in institutions could be more appropriately cared for in the community if a range of services were available. These services, interestingly enough, are not high technology health services. Although some nursing and physiotherapy, and other professional services, may be necessary home making, home maintenance, friendly visiting, shopping and transportation services are the most frequently requested. Most elderly do not want to enter institutions and prefer to remain in their own homes, but the necessary shift of expenditure from institutions to community-based services requires a major restructuring of the health-care system.

HEALTH EXPENDITURES

Present expenditures on health care are high and seem to be rising. As noted previously, it is inappropriate to attribute this rise in costs only to the elderly. The Economic Council of Canada states that, in terms of hospital admission rates, the change in the age structure of Canada has had little impact because at least three-quarters of hospital admissions came from younger age groups. Lower admissions of young women admitted for childbirth more than compensated for the greater influx of elderly patients. The net effect of demographic change, in hospital admissions, was close to zero. However, total health-care costs include long-term care in institutions and home care. Relative expenditures vary by province; see Tables 5.2 and 5.3 for Ontario as an example of cost distribution.

The increases in health-care costs are the results of new technology, the rising costs of services and goods and the increased

TABLE 5.1

Institutionalization of the Elderly, 1978-1982[1]

	U.S.[2] 1981 %	U.K.[3] 1982 %	Canada[4] 1978 %
65+	6.0	5.0	7.1
85+	25.0	21.0	31.0

1. Includes long-term institutional care. Excludes acute hospital care.
2. U.S. figures are approximate.
3. U.K. figures are approximate.
4. Wilkins, R. and Adams, O. *Healthfulness of Life*, The Institute for Research on Public Policy, Montreal, 1983

number of physicians for each person. It is difficult to obtain figures for Canada as a total since health is a provincial responsibility and there is considerable variation across the country. However, it is of some interest to explore the figures available (see Table 5.4).

In 1983, Ontario's Ministry of Health spent approximately 2.6 per cent of its total budget on home-care services (see Table 5.3). This is rather low compared to the amount spent on medical and institutional care. The belief that increased community services reduce costs is entirely impressionistic, and no study in North America has shown that increased home-care benefits would reduce institutionally-based costs. However, some small studies have suggested that a greater emphasis on home care

TABLE 5.2

Estimated Cost of Public Expenditures for the Elderly by all
Ministries in Ontario, 1982-1983
Applicable to those 65+

	Cost ($ millions)	% (total for all ages)
Ministry of Health	2,352	35.6
Ministry of Community & Social Affairs	180	
Homes for the Aged		
Home Support		
Treasury	280	
(OHIP Premium Workers)		
Revenue		
Tax Grant	350	
Gains	90	
Ministry of Municipal Affairs and Housing	80	
Total	3,332	14.5

Source: Seniors Secretariat, Ontario, unpublished data, 1983.

TABLE 5.3

Estimated Cost of Public Expenditures for the Elderly
by the Ministry of Health in Ontario, 1982-1983
Applicable to those 65+

	Cost ($ Millions)	% of total for all ages
Ministry of Health General Hospital (Invalid and outpatient)	1,100	38
Long Term	440	
Chronic Care		79
Extended Care		93
OHIP Benefits	340	19
Drug Benefits	185	95
Mental Hospitals	74	
Psychiatric Hospitals		15
Special Care		49
HomeCare	63	
Acute		56
Chronic		77
Other (Public Health, Ambulance, Community Health, etc.)	150	
Total	2,352	35.6

Source: Ontario Ministry of Health, unpublished documents, 1984.

could reduce visits to physicians and acute-care hospitalization, two factors that account for some of the highest costs for each unit. It has been pointed out that " ... efforts to constrain supply must occur independently of developing new resources in the community. The presence of a community care system provides an enabling environment in which to take deliberate political action." What is being suggested is not to turn individuals out of existing facilities, but to constrain the growth of high-cost and inappropriate institutional facilities by implementing community social supports that do not require professional services. It must also be ensured that community-based services are not seen as an abrogation of support to families. If 5 per cent of families caring for frail elderly withdrew care, the system would become overloaded. Accordingly, it is important to consider policies that support the care-giver and facilitate familial care-giving. A number of policies have been suggested, such as more tax rebate for household health care, respite care or paid time off from jobs.

If alternative health-care models are not tried, some very unpleasant decision-making will become necessary. For example, in Great Britain dialysis is not available to anyone over 55 within the national health-care system. Would we feel comfortable with the fact that, if someone is over 55 and has the money to pay for a procedure, it is available, but it is not available to someone who cannot pay? Is it right to allow bypass heart surgery at 64, but not at 66? When does one discontinue support systems? Who decides how and when? Moreover, as previously noted, health status is not easily defined by age, and it hardly seems sensible, let alone ethical, to penalize someone who has pursued a healthy life-style by withdrawing a service from them because they have delayed its incidence by sensible life-style choices. It is clear that the goals for health care must be defined and then the system structured to achieve those goals.

INFORMAL CARE-GIVERS

In spite of having one of the best health-care systems in the world, about 75 per cent of Canada's health care is provided by informal care-givers. For the older population, these are for the most part spouses (especially wives) daughters and daughters-

TABLE 5.4

Major Categories of Health Expenditures as Percentage of Total,
Canada, 1960-1982

	1960 %	1965 %	1970 %	1975 %	1980 %
General & allied hospitals	28	34	37	40	40
Physician	17	16	17	16	15
Homes & special care	14.5	13	12	11	12
Drugs & appliances	9	8	6	5	6
Dentists' services	6	6.5	8	9.5	13.5
Capital expenditures	5	4.5	4	5	6.5

Source: Health and Welfare Canada

in-law; for the young, they are, of course, parents. Except for the spouses of the elderly, most of the care-givers are middle-aged so that the 40 and over group gives care to the young and the needy old. In most cases the informal care-giver is a woman. With the changing roles of women and the fact that there is a continuing trend for more and more women to be in the labour market, it is appropriate to question whether this state of affairs can continue. What are the built-in social structures and attitudes that assume women should have this ongoing function?

Families are not likely to abandon their old, or sick and frail, but new initiatives will be needed to accommodate the effects of such changes as increased labour-market participation by women, multiple marriages and the larger variety of living arrangements. In view of these changes it has been suggested that the baby boomers, with fewer children or spouses available to be care-givers, will have to depend more on siblings and friends, or the formal system.

These changes raise issues about the need to develop a range of options so that there is some flexibility and support in the system to meet a wide range of needs. At present, women provide the bulk of volunteer services and low paid health service jobs. Volunteer work may have to be made more appealing to a wider range of individuals, particularly retirees, and especially retired men, and home care service jobs will need to offer appropriate remuneration and conditions.

INSTITUTIONAL CARE

Currently, institutional care is delivered in a variety of settings namely, acute-care hospitals, homes for the aged, retirement homes, nursing homes and chronic-care hospitals. A difficult problem in this area is how to set up assessment to evaluate the many factors and conditions that contribute to illness, and result in planning suitably tailored to individual needs. In addition, there are the problems of managing resources, having a range of appropriate options and making them available and accessible.

One of the most significant demographic facts is the rapid increase in the survival of the very old. The 85 and over group has doubled in the past ten years, and will probably double again by the year 2001. This age group, the old-old, are at high risk for institutionalization. These people are also more prone to use the acute-care hospital for the last days of their lives (a practice that accounts for a high proportion of health-care costs), and for stays that are often prolonged because of lack of alternative community resources. A typical case might be that of an 85 year old woman, widowed and living alone who, because of either unstable blood pressure, a badly placed scatter rug, or osteoporosis, falls and fractures a hip. The acute phase requires surgery, then convalescence, followed by rehabilitation, and, if all goes well, her return to the community. However, her recovery will be slow and it may be impossible for her to return to living completely on her own at home. It is also likely that there may not be an appropriate rehabilitation programme geared for this type of patient. An appropriate placement in an assisted environment may not be possible because of the paucity of such housing units. She may either remain in the acute-care hospital, or be placed in a nursing home or chronic-care hospital at a higher level of care than necessary. Both solutions are inappropriate, but may be inevitable if a range of options is not available. The acute-care hospital is not equipped to deal with long-term care, and the unstimulating, crisis-oriented care often results in deterioration of the individual so that he or she becomes more dependent and in need of more intense care. In a long-term care institution, where care is not likely tailored towards rehabilitation or to a higher quality of life, dependency may be encouraged and ultimately result in an increased need for health care.

Although classification of long-term care institutions varies from province to province, overall similarities are to be found. In Ontario, long-term care institutions are assigned to one of four classifications: providing residential supervision (retirement homes, homes for the aged); nursing homes (those that require one and a half hours a day of nursing care); extended-care facilities for those requiring intense nursing care; and chronic-care hospitals for those requiring significant medical interventions as well as intense nursing care. What is now happening is that the actual need for, and use of, these facilities is changing.

The shift to increased community-based services, which reflects the desire of most elderly to remain in their own homes as long as possible, has led to a decrease in the number of residents requiring simple, daily supervision. At the same time, however, both homes for the aged and nursing homes have a high percentage of residents requiring extended care; that is, heavy nursing care of probably more than one and a half hours a day. The average age in these facilities across the country ranges from about 83 to 87.

There are some major difficulties concerning the appropriate placement of the elderly in homes for the aged and nursing homes. A private nursing home can attempt to limit the number of patients needing a great deal of care and insist that such patients be transferred to other facilities as their need for care increases. Manitoba has probably gone the farthest in developing an integrated assessment and placement system.

Government, for the most part, sets standards for homes for the aged and nursing homes. However, these standards tend to be monitored mostly for physical factors such as fire hazards, staff to patient ratio, and space, but with little attention to quality of life, or quality of personnel. In some provinces, for instance Ontario, homes for the aged and nursing homes are the responsibility of two different ministries, whereas in others, for instance Manitoba, there is a more integrated and co-ordinated system. A further problem is the unnecessary shifting of residents that occurs because certain commonly used medical procedures are not permitted in nursing homes. Patients in need of treatment may be summarily transferred to acute- or chronic-care hospitals. However, with medical consultation available and properly trained nurses, many straightforward procedures could be carried out in the nursing home or homes for the aged. Inflexible funding structures and regulations tend to lie at the root of this problem.

The present wide variety of levels of care may no longer be appropriate. Implementation of a system that gives a continuum of care in one institutional setting would avoid the uncertainties and stress associated with the present system. Such a system would have to offer a variety of housing options (see Chapter 6). Housing options, augmented by well organized and co-ordinated community services and regional geriatric assessment units, would radically reduce the need for increased numbers of long-term institutions. Surveys indicate that, if services were available and accessible, 15 to 20 per cent of residents now in long-term care institutions could be cared for in the community.

Few cost-effectiveness studies have been done, but there is some evidence that community care may or may not be less costly, but would definitely be more effective. However, we should not rush into deinstitutionalization before community-based support services are in place. It is crucial to learn from previous mistakes in the mental health field where psychiatric patients were discharged from hospitals without appropriate community-support services in existence.

Innovative methods of delivering health care, both in terms of health promotion and the locus of delivery, will be of importance in changing the rate of institutionalization. Since a significant proportion of institutional costs occur for the care of terminal illness, the whole question of palliative care may need further study. Increased numbers of palliative care units and palliative home care should come under consideration.

DENTAL CARE

An aspect of the health-care system, very often overlooked, is dental health and hygiene. Dental health is important since with increasing age, oral hygiene and dental care not only affect self-image, but also the quality of an individual's nutrition. There is already a marked change in the dental health of the population and the present middle-aged and "young-old" are different from previous generations in that a high proportion retain their own teeth. As a result, the over-40 generation uses dentists and dental hygienists to maintain their teeth and to deal with changes in bone structure and in the gums around the teeth. This requires a shift in the knowledge and practice of dental practitioners. The present generation of elderly, and particularly the very elderly, have had most of their teeth replaced by dentures. These must be properly maintained and fitted on a regular basis as the structure of the mouth changes. Properly fitted and maintained dentures are important for adequate diet and for personal appearance. Many elderly are embarrassed and withdraw from social contact because of poorly fitting dentures. There are many stories of dentures sitting in cups, rather than in the mouth. In institutions, many personal crises arise when dentures are accidentally thrown into the garbage.

There will be an increased need to look at efficient and effective ways of providing dental care. Dental care is not presently covered by the universal health insurance plans and, therefore, use is often determined by ability to pay.

USE OF MEDICATIONS AND DRUGS

One of the most important concerns is the high usage of prescribed and over-the-counter (OTC) drugs. There is a tendency in our society as a whole to seek help from drugs. The elderly, however, consume high proportions of both prescribed and OTC drugs. This is the result of a number of factors, one of which is the high incidence of chronic conditions among older people. The elderly are also more prone to treat minor ailments with self-administered medication, rather than alternative methods. For example, older people tend to use laxatives to treat constipation rather than adopt an appropriate diet and take adequate exercise. And if you suffer from mild joint stiffness, or if you have a headache, it is probably easier to take a pill rather than change your shoes, or put on your coat and go for a walk in the fresh air.

Another factor that contributes to overuse of drugs is the expectation, by many individuals, that every ailment can be quickly cured by medication. There is also a tendency for physicians to reinforce this view and to attempt to meet these expectations. There is some suggestion that drug benefit programmes, while enabling individuals to afford necessary medication, facilitate the use of drugs when other responses might be more appropriate.

Lack of information about normal physiological changes associated with aging has been identified as another factor contributing to overuse of medication. Sleep patterns change in later life, but individuals still expect to sleep approximately eight uninterrupted hours a night and seek, and use, sleep sedation excessively. Tranquillizers tend to be overused and overprescribed in the general population, especially to women, but these medications may have particularly serious side effects for older individuals.

Furthermore, the need for some people to take more than one medication at a time is made more difficult and hazardous by being inadequately monitored. The prescription of a harmful combination of drugs is fairly common, since often more than one prescribing physician is involved. Re-organization is again the key. Sufficient time must be allocated for adequate history-taking, assessment and follow-up if the current situation is to be improved. Accurate monitoring systems need to be developed and universally used to detect inappropriate drug combinations and, perhaps, their likely consequences.

MENTAL HEALTH

Care for older adults with mental health problems is limited. However, older adults now constitute the majority of patients in psychiatric hospitals. Nursing homes house many patients suffering from dementia, and do not have staff or facilities for special care. Moreover, only recently has there been a growing recognition of the wide range of mental health problems suffered by the elderly: problems such as mild to severe depression and anxiety or other neuroses, which were previously poorly diagnosed and frequently not treated. This was due partly to a lack of understanding of these conditions and their manifestations in later years, and to the belief by health-care professionals that many of the symptoms were inevitable with aging, and in any case not treatable. The problem has been exacerbated by the fact that the elderly themselves have felt ashamed of consulting psychiatrists or psychologists for fear of being labelled "crazy." Consequently, the mental health sector has been neglected in terms of availability and accessibility of services for the over-50 group. The high rate of suicide in men over age 60 and the problem of later-life alcoholism are indicators of the seriousness of the problem. The field of geriatric psychiatry is growing, however, and new outreach community-based multidisciplinary teams are being developed so that the elderly can be assessed more adequately in their homes. This has led to a broader assessment system that, it is hoped, will reduce unnecessary institutionalization since the total situation is considered, and there is the opportunity to give informal care-givers the support they need. It must be stressed that the promotion of good mental health requires an appreciation of the total life situation which may confront the elderly.

SELF-HELP AND SUPPORT GROUPS

There is no question that as the elderly become better educated, healthier, more active and wealthier, the trend towards self-help and support groups will increase. In the context of health promotion and disease prevention, there is and will be greater emphasis on individuals taking more responsibility for their own health. The non-smoking public policy has been one step in trying to get individuals to change their behaviour. We can further improve our health by not drinking excessively, by using medication properly and by paying attention to our nutritional and excerise needs. The role of informal and formal support groups in contributing to health and well-being is frequently not recognized. Informal support groups consist of family, friends and social groups that can be called in time of need, or who are there to help exchange information or confidences, who help make leisure activities pleasurable and who generally contribute to our sense of worth and well-being. Everyone needs to feel someone cares, and studies have shown that having at least one confidant, and a supportive social network, is extremely important in maintaining and increasing a person's mental and physical capacities.

More formal support groups have been organized to help individuals around crisis situations or difficult life transitions. The best known of these is Alcoholics Anonymous, but such support groups as those dealing with dismissal from a job, retirement, widowhood and family violence, among others, have also proved beneficial in helping individuals cope more effectively. Health care involves stress management as well as life-style counselling or change.

OTHER ISSUES IN HEALTH CARE

Ethnicity and Multiculturalism

Canada is frequently referred to as a "mosaic" — a society consisting of a great number and wide range of ethnic and culturally diverse groups. An active immigration programme ensures a constant flow of new immigrants, and recent changes in immigration policy have led to the entry in Canada of a larger number of older immigrants than previously. This results in increased numbers of individuals, both old and young, who need and will continue to need health care, but who have difficulty in gaining access to the health-care system because of language and cultural barriers. Many elderly immigrants do not learn English or French and are thus extremely dependent on their children to act as intermediaries in the system. In some areas, translators are provided and some attention has been paid to this concern, but overall it remains a problem. It is particularly relevant to long-term care situations, both in terms of community-based services and institutions. Some provinces, such as Ontario, have a policy of encouraging ethnic homes and nursing homes for the elderly and in cities, such as Toronto, a number of ethnic communities have established homes catering to particular ethnic or religious groups. There is evidence that older individuals are happier in homes where they can continue their ethnic, cultural and religious practices. Obviously, not only is it important to be able to converse in one's native language, but also to be able to eat familiar food, and to have the opportunity to interact, on an on-going basis, with individuals who share a common history and often have shared memories. This also underlines the need for staff who communicate with the residents in a common language.

In community-based situations, although the need for communication in a language that is understood is critical, a need for "cultural" understanding is equally important. An example of this concerns an elderly Portuguese woman who was diagnosed as having later-life diabetes, which the physician felt should be controlled by diet. However, when simply presented with a list of foods not to be eaten the woman felt that she must be dying as the list forbade many of the foods that were an integral part of her normal diet. A nutritionist was consulted who understood the cultural significance attached to certain foods by this particular woman and the diet was adjusted, which overcame the patient's extreme anxiety associated with the diagnosis and her fear of starving to death.

Education and Training of Health-Care Professionals

Education is needed both for the public and for health-care professionals to promote better understanding of what can be expected from the aging process itself, and what can be done to promote health and well-being. There is a need for public education programmes and for realistic portrayal of aging in the media in primary and secondary schools. There is also a pressing need to train professionals to deliver health and social services to an aging population and to the very elderly. Only recently have medical schools started to introduce undergraduate courses on the aging process and on the multidisciplinary care of the elderly (gerontology and geriatrics). Similarly, nursing, occupational therapy, physiotherapy, speech therapy, pharmacy, dentistry and social work have just begun to place some emphasis on training at the undergraduate level in the area of aging and old age. At the graduate level, residency training has existed for the past 10 years or more, but it is spotty across the country and does not cover the range of health-care professionals necessary to assure the quality of service that Canadians have been led to expect.

There is a significant shortage of appropriately trained health- and social-service professionals in the field of geriatrics and gerontology, and policies are needed to foster that training. A critical element in meeting this need is well-qualified teachers and faculty.

Continuing education is also extremely important since a great deal of care is being delivered by professionals who have had little or no training to deal with the many complex problems of the old and very old. An example is the family physician who is, for most older people, the first contact for primary care. Family physicians have limited time, they are frequently untrained in caring for the elderly, and are often unfamiliar with the community resources that would be helpful in keeping an elderly person a healthy and productive member of the community. Adjustments in pay schedules for services to older patients, such as for home-visits and longer assessments, should be investigated.

Research

The discussion of health-care issues cannot be concluded without a word about research.

Canada spends less on basic and applied research than most western countries. Furthermore, there has been poor collection of data on the incidence and prevalence of various diseases and conditions in Canada. Some of this material is now being gathered, but an accessible comprehensive data base is necessary.

There is some movement now in identifying research in aging, and old age as a priority. However, it is still an area that is inadequately funded, and some of the granting agencies have been slow to set up appropriate multidisciplinary committees on aging for reviewing research proposals. The federal government has begun to identify diseases of old age that need special attention, such as senile dementia of the Alzheimer-type and osteoporosis. But there is little recognition of the need for a better understanding of the underlying factors that interact to produce poor mental and physical health, and that would give greater substance to the framework of health promotion. Evaluation of existing programmes has also not been as general as necessary. The relative importance and interactions among income security, housing conditions and options, ethnicity, family structure, stress, work place safety, social networks, leisure activities, and behaviour and health, are just a sample of the critical areas needing investigation and yet provide an almost overwhelming list.

An issue that cannot be overlooked in this field particularly is the need to bridge the gap between research and practice. There is already considerable information based on sound research, but it is necessary for practitioners to be trained to know where to look for the information and to have the skill to assess the adequacy and relevance of the information. The information must be disseminated in a form that will reach the practitioner in a meaningful way.

Lastly, it is impossible to ignore the issue of territoriality. Particularly in an interdisciplinary field such as health care for the elderly, the natural tendency of vested interests to maintain the status quo must be recognized and overcome. This is of importance since the health-care delivery system requires radical reorganization, both to meet the needs of an aging population more appropriately, and to contain costs.

6

HOUSING

Although health and social services are readily seen as major issues in the case of an aging population, housing is often not perceived as a related element. Yet, since it is generally agreed that a person's well-being, self esteem and sense of identity are significantly influenced by physical surroundings, the range and appropriateness of housing available for the elderly is clearly very important.

This chapter examines where, and how, Canada's current older population is housed, what options are open as an individual gets older and how available and appropriate these options are. In addition, it explores in what way the needs of the future elderly will differ from those of today, and highlights some of the factors that appear to militate against the provision of appropriate and accessible shelter for all members of our society.

EARLY RETIREMENT HOUSING ISSUES AND PROBLEMS

At the outset, it should be noted that, as the baby-boom generation ages, there is likely to be considerable activity in the pre-retirement housing market over the 1990s and beyond. Since most people tend to stay in their residential accommodation until at least retirement age, this does not signal a dramatic reversal in current housing trends. However, with the leading edge of the baby boom having entered their 40s in the middle of the 1980s there will be increased emphasis on those housing options that adequately reflect the "empty nest" reality — reduction in family size as a result of children leaving home. These options will involve reduced house size, relocation to be near where children settle or changing housing characteristics (one-storey, or ground floor, accommodation). For many of the baby-boom generation, there will be no change in housing status until they become elderly, but for those who do exercise the new options there will be significantly more appropriate housing available at the turn of the century than there was a decade earlier. Consequently, the traditional housing market is likely to be oriented towards satisfying the young baby boomers until the middle of the 1990s, at which time there is likely to be a significant reorientation to the older generation including the increasing numbers of pre- and early-retirees, and the elderly. It is useful to keep this perspective in mind when options for the elderly are outlined in the sections that follow.

There is now a growing concern in parts of Canada about the lack of adequate housing. Although supply levels vary widely across the country, in many urban areas there is a shortage. Rising prices appear to be a major factor in this shortage since it is more a shortage of affordable and accessible housing, than of housing stock. Younger adults are finding it increasingly difficult to purchase a home because of soaring prices. This puts pressure on the rental market and drives up prices in that sector. And this, in turn, creates problems for people at the lower end of the income scale. For the most part, these people are the unemployed, the working poor, the increasing number of individuals who find themselves single parents, and the elderly. The majority are women. A relatively recent phenomenon is the increasing number of individuals who are forced to take early retirement, many at a time when they still have family responsibilities and may still be paying off a mortgage.

Think about John D., 52 years old, who has two children at university and a house to pay off, and who has become accustomed to a middle-class standard of living. John is laid off due to corporate reorganization or merger. He may be given severance pay, but he faces the difficult task of finding work at age 52 when the corporate world, and industry, tends to classify anyone over 45 as "old." If John does not re-enter the work force, he is faced with various stresses that can lead to marriage break-down, alcoholism and other problems.

It has been suggested that with fewer young children we can shift some resources — those used for education, for example — to meet the housing or health needs of older generations. In fact, that does not seem easy to do, and care has to be exercised about such options as turning schools into housing for seniors. The housing that results from such schemes may be second-rate or not economically viable.

In Canada, the implementation of public policy in the field of housing has been made even more difficult because in most regions of the country three levels of government are involved: municipal, provincial and federal. In addition, even within each level, there has been little collaboration between ministries that overlap — for instance, ministries of transportation, revenue, health and social services.

What is known, however, is that taking into account all the governmental expenditures on all programmes for the elderly, there is a discouragingly small percentage for housing. The following figures for one province (Ontario 1984/85) serve as a vivid example of the deficiency in resource allocation. Provincial Government Expenditures for Seniors' Services were:

48% -hospital and medical health care
20% -long-term institutional care
19% -income support
12% -shelter and home support

The 12 per cent represents the total spent to keep seniors at home. This amount can be further broken down. Of the 12 per cent:

7% -home maintenance and property tax grants
15% -assisted independent living units

16% -home support services
2% -innovative semi-independent housing

Thus, in 1984-85, innovative semi-independent housing received 2 per cent of 12 per cent of $3.9 billion, or less than $1 million. By 1986-87 this amount was increased, but only to between $3 million and $4 million. Furthermore, if the national housing type figures are compared to those of Sweden and the Netherlands, the minimal emphasis Canada puts on providing supported housing for the elderly is apparent (see Table 6.1).

TABLE 6.1

Distribution of Elderly (65+) in Canada, Sweden and the
Netherlands by Housing Type

	Canada %	Sweden %	Netherlands %
Independent living	87.5	80.9	72.0
Supported independent	5.9	15.6	23.5
Dependent living	6.6	3.5	4.5

Although the Canadian provinces show some differences, the pattern tends to be similar.

Source: Brink, Satya "Housing Elderly People in Canada," in Gutman, G. and Blackie, N. (eds.), *Innovations in Housing and Living Arrangements for Seniors (1985), Simon Fraser University.*

Tenure

A high proportion of Canada's population are homeowners. About 60 per cent of the adult population own their own home; for those over 65, the rate is slightly higher, at 66 per cent. Older homeowners also tend to have paid off their mortgages, and Statistics Canada reported in 1982 that six out of 10 household heads aged 65 and over owned their homes mortgage free. Although the percentage of homeowners decreases as age increases, in 1982, even in the 80 and over group, 56 per cent owned their own home.

Living Arrangements

Most of the older population (two out of three) live in family settings, either with a spouse or with their children. However, because of their longer life expectancy, and their likelihood of becoming widowed, the proportion of elderly women living in family settings decreases rapidly with age. Among women over the age of 75, 36 per cent live alone in private households, and 20 per cent live as residents of collect dwellings. The figures for men in the same age group are 16 per cent and 13 per cent respectively (see Table 6.2).

TABLE 6.2

Distribution of Living Arrangements of Persons 65+ and 85+ by Sex, Canada, 1981

Living Arrangements	65+		85+	
	Male %	Female %	Male %	Female %
Private Household				
Living alone	13.0	32.4	16.6	25.5
With spouse only	53.2	29.8	28.1	4.3
With non-relatives	2.6	2.5	3.1	2.2
With family or other relatives	24.6	24.9	23.3	26.9
Collective Households				
In Nursing Homes and Institutions for Elderly chronically ill	4.7	8.2	24.8	36.3
In hospitals	0.8	0.9	2.8	3.0
In other collective households	1.0	1.4	1.3	1.8

Source: Statistics Canada, census 1981.

Income and Housing
Housing choices are largely tied to the level of available income
and the 1981 Census figures show that the monetary incomes of
older people tend to be concentrated at the lower end of the scale.
Elderly unattached individuals are the most likely to be in the
low groups, with single women having a lower income than
single men. Nevertheless, incomes for this age group have increased proportionately and significantly over the last ten years
and can be expected to improve for future groups (see Table 6.3).

The above statistics suggest the following conclusions. Married people are more likely than those divorced or widowed to

TABLE 6.3

Incidence of Low Income (1978 basis) by Age among Families
and Unattached Individuals, Canada

Families by age of head	1979	1984
24 and under	20.5	30.1
25-34	12.4	17.7
35-44	10.9	13.1
45-54	9.4	11.3
55-64	12.3	12.8
65+	21.9	11.4
Total	13.1	14.5
Individuals by Age:		
24 and under	37.2	47.1
25-34	17.4	21.2
35-44	21.8	26.1
45-54	32.5	33.6
55-65	43.5	44.0
65+	66.3	49.6
Total	40.3	37.8

Source: Statistics Canada, Census 1986.

own homes and live in a house. The person aged 70 and over, who lives alone, is most likely to be a widowed, divorced or never-married woman. She will tend to have a lower income than her male counterpart and will probably live in rented accommodation. There is a strong possibliity that she will be forced, by necessity, to move from a familiar area to one where she no longer feels a familiarity with neighbours. Ultimately, she may be faced with institutionalization as the only viable option.

The very old single person, therefore, is vulnerable to the possibility of becoming isolated, particularly as he or she is increasingly likely to suffer from chronic health problems such as arthritis and declining vision and hearing. Even in situations where both spouses survive, there may be difficulties. Until recently, even if people wanted to move, there have been few housing options open to the elderly; thus, there has been little incentive to sell a home that may have become too large or too inconvenient.

Barriers to Moving for the Elderly

In addition to the paucity of alternative convenient, affordable and appropriate housing choices for the elderly, there are other barriers to moving. Fear is one. Apart from subsidized rental housing geared to income, which is in short supply, home ownership provides the best protection against inflation. Older people, moreover, find it difficult to leave familiar surroundings, and many elderly will reduce their other expenses, even to the point of endangering their health, in order to maintain their home in an area they are used to.

This has meant that many elderly have an asset that does not benefit them in terms of their standard of living — their cash income may be lower than necessary. There have been a number of home-equity conversion plans suggested that would allow owners to remain in their own homes if they so desire, but increase their cash flow. One is the "reverse mortgage," in which a lender provides the homeowner with a loan against some of the equity in the house. The loan may be either a lump sum that the homeowner uses to purchase an annuity, or monthly payments (called a rising debt loan). In both cases the house serves as collateral and accrued interest need not be paid until after a specified term. The underlying assumption is that the home will eventually be sold to retire the debt, any surplus money going to the homeowner or, in the case of the elderly, usually to the homeowner's estate. A second approach is a "sale-lease back plan" in which an investor buys a home and then leases it back to the former owner for life. The seller usually receives a lump sum down payment plus monthly payments. The new owner assumes all expenses such as taxes, insurance, major repairs and negotiates the rent payable by the previous owner. A third approach involves "deferred-payment loans" that are usually made to the homeowner for a specific purpose, such as modernizing or rehabilitating the house. Repayment is usually not due until the owner dies, or the house is sold.

To date, none of these plans has been very attractive to older homeowners, or to financial institutions, in Canada. For many, the home is the one source of security and their only asset to pass on as a legacy to their children. This seems to be a factor of considerable psychological importance to the present elderly, but may change for future generations.

SHELTER FOR THE OLD AND VERY OLD

To date, there have been fairly limited options for housing and living arrangements. The predominant pattern has been for people to buy a single family home when they marry and start a family, and the present elderly have tended to stay in their own single family dwellings from 15 to 30 years or more. The trend among those now middle aged has been to "trade up" from modest homes to bigger, more expensive homes. The tendency for the majority, particularly for married couples, has been to remain in their own mortgage-free homes. However, now there are an increasing number of choices. First, for those who do not choose, or are not forced, to move, there are the three home equity conversion plans mentioned above, namely, reverse mortgages, sale-leaseback and deferred-payment loans. As these options are often complex, professional, financial and legal assistance are often needed so the implications are well understood.

Many older adults do, however, wish to make a change in their housing arrangements, either because of health and economic status, or because of other factors such as the loss of spouse, or the desire to be closer to children. A further reason, common in Canada, is the desire to move full- or part-time to a warmer climate.

The decision to move is a very critical one for the older adult, and should be carefully considered. Still, many individuals have made voluntary moves that have enhanced their quality of life. The two most important factors in prompting the decision to move are increasing difficulty in performing the tasks of daily living, and increased social isolation.

Options

Garden suites, accessory apartments, flexible housing and bi-family units are all options to maintain independent living that allow the elderly person to live close to relatives or friends in a mutually supportive way. Garden suites and accessory apartments are usually small structures erected in the garden of a house, or attached to the house. They usually consist of a living area, bedroom, kitchen and bathroom. Flexible and bi-family housing usually involves the conversion of a larger home into smaller units, sometimes with the use of common areas for living and dining. These options often involve changes in zoning by-laws, which can present some difficulties. The so-called "granny-flats," which have been fairly popular in Australia, require large lots and receptive communities, and although they have been tried in some communities, they have not been particularly appealing to Canadians.

Home-sharing is another option, and some communities have "non-profit" agencies that keep a register of those who wish to share their home, and attempt to match a suitable applicant. This has worked fairly well for some individuals. Home-sharing with someone of one's own age, or with a younger person, has been successful in helping to alleviate loneliness, or the costs and labour involved in maintaining a home. Problems may arise, however, because one person is always in the position of sharing the owner's home and this places that person in an unequal position. The success is often dependent on the personality and flexibility of the individuals involved.

Congregate housing is a term that covers the sharing of a home in which none of the individuals owns the house, but all contribute to its upkeep. Each individual has private quarters, even though communal facilities and main meals are usually shared. Great Britain has pioneered the sheltered housing concept in which there is a live-in housekeeper who attends to the daily running of the house, and can handle emergency situations by liaison with the appropriate community agency. One form of these housing options — known as the Abbeyfield Concept — involves small groups living in a home-like atmosphere, mostly in converted houses.

Life-care communities are another option being developed, often by private entrepreneurs, but also by religious and ethnic groups. These usually involve high-rise towers of independent apartments with access to activity areas; they may have dining facilities. Many have some staff on call for handling emergencies and day-to-day crises. Some have a nearby, or attached, nursing home available should the resident no longer be able to carry on independently. Each community has its own method of payment, services offered and regulations regarding transfers.

A variety of retirement communities are now in existence. These are primarily geared to the young-old, or over-50 group who are retired, but wish to pursue an active life-style. There are new-towns that tend to be rather large, such as Arizona's Sun

City or California's Leisure World, which have from 22,000 to 47,000 residents. These towns have single dwellings, town houses and high-rise buildings, tend to have a range of facilities and businesses and are generally self-contained. There are none of this scale in Canada.

Retirement-villages tend to be smaller and offer a wide assortment of leisure and recreational activities. Although not self-contained, they are segregated and offer security. Retirement subdivisions are privately built residential environments for a predominantly elderly population, but have few facilities. Consequently, they are often built close to shopping, transportation and other amenities in the surrounding community. Some of these subdivisions are of the mobile-home-type. A number of this type of village exist in Canada.

Retirement residences, which may be built for profit or non-profit by churches and ethnic groups, provide a protected, but somewhat independent environment. Private suites are usually the format, with shared recreational space and meals provided if desired.

There are a significant number of the early (50+) retirees who spend a part of the year in the south avoiding Canada's cold months. Most tend to go to Florida, Arizona and California and, for the most part, do not stay longer than six months less a day, in order to maintain their Canadian residence and eligibility for access to the universal medical care. Some sell their homes in urban centres and have two leisure homes. There has been some migration within Canada to the milder climate of the west coast, particularly to Victoria, British Columbia.

Any permanent move should be carefully considered, and it is usually wise to rent and spend some time in a new environment to see how realistic one's expectations are. Economic implications should also be carefully reviewed.

Having two leisure homes, or migrating to the southern United States is usually a pattern among the "young-old" — those up to age 75 or so. The older individuals (80+) tend to be less mobile and tend to be found in highest proportions in urban areas. This is due in part to the fact that in very late life one is more likely to be single, less likely to be driving an automobile and more likely to need some support and health services.

SOME DILEMMAS AND DIFFICULTIES

One issue in housing for the elderly, which remains predominant, is the debate about the relative merits of age-segregated housing and integrated housing. Those in favour of integrated housing decry an environment with only older people. In contrast, those who support age-segregation argue that without specially designed environments, and provision of affordable housing, the needs of the elderly will be neglected. Some studies have found that residents of age-segregated housing have higher survival rates than those in age-integrated housing. Other studies have suggested that as people tend to form friendships most readily with peers, the elderly are therefore happier in age-segregated environments. One must be careful, however, since most studies do not carefully make allowances for the health and social status of the residents.

The answer is clearly to ensure that the individual has a variety of choices and options in later life. It is clear that programmes of adequate shelter allowances, which take into account regional differences, will need to be implemented in order to bring about widely accessible and realistic choices. The term "shelter allowances" means giving direct payments to people so that they can afford available alternatives. However, administering and controlling such programmes is difficult and governments are wary.

There has also been a continuing debate between government and other groups involved in housing development, and those that deliver health and social services. The housing suppliers argue that the provision of services in housing developments turns them into nursing homes; the health and social-services

sector replies that without such services the housing developments are not meeting the needs of those who are expected to
live in them. Clearly some form of compromise must be found
since individuals entering a housing situation do age, and with
increasing age may have increased need for support. Recently,
the concept of assisted independent living, which fosters the co-
ordination and delivery of some services to tenants who live for
the most part independently, has been introduced. It has been
shown that having someone who can intervene in crises, to
provide some services such as shopping or meals over the short
term, some security checks, or a community health clinic located
on the premises delays institutionalization and reduces
physicians' visits and the use of acute-care hospitals.

Environmental Design
Environmental design is a planning concept that needs greater
emphasis. The inclusion of more barrier-free buildings in settings for an aging population is an important consideration.
Canada has been slow in providing housing designed for handicapped people and in assuring the availability of devices to
enable individuals to live independently. There should be the
provision of a greater number of units that have doors wide
enough for a wheelchair and bathrooms large enough to accommodate a wheelchair. Bathrooms and kitchens generally are not
equipped for use by the handicapped. Grab bars in the bathroom,
adjustable counters in the kitchen, proper lighting and floor
covering, are all frequently overlooked. The future will probably require that strategies to accommodate disabilities such as impaired vision and hearing, arthritic fingers, or confinement to a
wheelchair, should be aesthetically incorporated into the built
environment. There should be increased attention to low cost
technologies that can be regarded as aids to independent living.
The technologically-sophisticated baby-boom generation will
certainly make demands for such aids in the future.
    Homes for the aged, nursing homes and chronic-care hospi-

tals are "home" for long-term care residents. Yet in these institutions there has been very little attention devoted to the impact of the physical environment on well-being. Physical surroundings that facilitate mobility and independence are important for everyone, but are particularly relevant for very old adults who are more likely to be impaired. Non-glare surfaces, telephones with flashing lights, taps that turn easily, flooring that does not increase the incidence of falls, furniture that is high enough to get in and out of easily, windows low enough to see out of, and interior decoration that is pleasing to the eye, are all important aspects of the built environment. The ability to spend time out of doors in a protected environment, or the availability of transportation, all play an important part in maintaining morale.

HOUSING THE FUTURE ELDERLY

So far we have discussed the situation of the present elderly, but what will it be like in the year 2001 or 2030 when the present baby boomers are old? While predictions should always be treated with caution, the ones that we make about our future elderly population may be more accurate than most because the population we are concerned with is already in early adulthood and manifests distinct characteristics that will affect their needs and demands in housing in later life.

For instance, we know that a greater number of people will have more money because they will have contributed to pension plans. At the same time, because women are entering the labour market in greater numbers and staying in it for a greater proportion of their lives, they will have better incomes. They also will be more accustomed to making their own decisions and living independently. Both men and women will be more demanding, but their family structures will not have been as stable. Changing life-styles, such as later marriages, higher divorce rates and multiple marriages, later parenting and greater geographic mobility, will all influence what their later life households and networks are likely to be. Thus, as the baby boomers move through middle age and old age, they will have different expectations as well as different personal and material resources, than their parents, the present elderly.

DISCERNING CONSUMERS

Among today's seniors, some are overhoused, while an even greater number have difficulty finding suitable housing that is affordable, accessible and appropriate. There has been, and still is, a tendency to regard seniors as a passive group, willing to accept the status of "invisible," second-class citizens. Seniors today, however, are a more discerning and vocal group than their predecessors, and we must plan ahead for an even more demanding and vocal group who will not accept this status. Fortunately, it is likely that this future group will have greater personal and financial resources to help meet their needs and expectations. The challenge is to provide the incentives to foster a variety of options since the aging of the population creates significantly changing needs at different times in life. As of yet, policies have not been developed, or put in place, that will better match housing to changing population needs, and also assure shelter for all members of the community.

7

ECONOMICS AND POLITICS

An aging society can be expected to have a significant impact on the functioning of the economic marketplace and the "marketplace" for votes. The consumption patterns of both private and public goods and services vary widely by age and, hence, the over-40 generation is likely to demand noticeably different goods and services than its predecessors. It is tempting to contrast the demands for health and education in this context. The popular view of an aging society might project reduced demand in the future for education and education-related goods and services, and an increased demand for health care and health-care related goods and services. This reflects the perception that as individuals we tend to acquire our education early in life to prepare us to be productive members of society over our subsequent lifetime, while we tend to need greater amounts of health care later in life when our bodies wear out and we are less able to look after ourselves. Of course, the distinction is not entirely accurate. Education, as has been noted in Chapter 4, is likely to become increasingly a lifelong process, while debilitating and expensive medical emergencies such as strokes and heart attacks are by no means limited to the later years. In the aggregate, however, there is some legitimacy to the general perception that appropriate policy for an aging society is the gradual transfer of resources from education-related to health-related activities.

This point has implications for the types of products that will be produced for both private and public consumption. In the private marketplace, preferences are expressed with dollars —

those items that are in demand will thrive, while those for which purchases are few will wither and ultimately die. In the public "marketplace" where preferences are expressed with votes, those political parties offering, and ultimately providing, the policy or package of policies that are in demand are likely to thrive politically (and probably economically as well), while those whose packages do not quite measure up will have a more difficult time garnishing votes (and dollars).

This chapter again uses the demographic framework as a basis for analysis and speculation regarding future trends in both the economic and political "marketplaces." These trends certainly have important implications not only for the type of society we live in, but also for the organizations and individuals producing the products.

DEMOGRAPHIC TRENDS

As a basis for this analysis consider the demographic trends summarized in Table 7.1. Over the 1970s (1971-81) the population grew by almost 13 per cent. However, this growth was unevenly spread over the age categories. Because of declining fertility, the pre-working-age young actually declined in numbers over the decade, and as a result producers of childrens' toys and other child-related products generally had a difficult time. On the other hand, those producing for the youth market (aged 15 to 24) were doing quite well, since population in these age categories was growing somewhat above the overall population growth. Moreover, it was in the 15 to 24 age group where the bulk of the baby-boom generation was located, so there were large numbers of people in these age groups. The real engine for growth was the leading edge of the baby boom — those people born in the late 1940s and early 1950s. This group grew almost 46 per cent over the 1970s, that is, at three and a half times the overall population growth rate. Products oriented towards this age group, such as pet foods, excelled in growth performance.

Population growth in the 35 to 44 age group was similar in magnitude to the youth market — somewhat above average — whereas growth in the 45 to 54 age group was the lowest of the older age groups. These are the people born around the depression of the 1930s, and there simply are not many of them. However, population growth was quite rapid over the "Roaring Twenties" and this is reflected in the almost 25 per cent growth rate in the pre-retirement group aged 55 to 64 years. In addition, increasing life expectancy results in ever increasing numbers of seniors and this group, as almost everyone is aware, grew a substantial 35 per cent over the 1970s. Products oriented towards this market did very well.

Demographic projections are based on the tautology that "every year we get a year older." Consequently, ten years later — over the 1980s — it is logical to expect the growth of the age groups experienced in the 1970s to be reflected in the growth of the age groups ten years their senior. This is apparent from the data in Table 7.1 where, for example, the numbers in the second

TABLE 7.1

Canadian Population Growth by Age, 1971-1991
%

Age	1971-1981[1]	1981-1991[2]	1991-2001[2]
0-14	-14.1	5.2	-4.1
15-24	16.4	-19.6	-0.7
25-34	45.9	15.8	-18.3
35-44	17.5	43.4	12.9
45-54	9.0	15.8	41.9
55-64	24.7	7.5	17.0
65 and Over	35.3	30.3	22.4
Total	12.9	10.6	6.5

[1] Actual.
[2] Projections by the authors.
Source: Statistics Canada and projections by the authors.

column of the table (the 1980s) reflect those in the first column (the 1970s) moved down one slot (that is, aged ten years).

Consider, for example, the youth age group. Above average growth over the 1970s has been replaced by absolute decline over the 1980s. The youth are rapidly becoming a "dying breed." However, this simply reflects the growth of the pre-youth group (under 14 years old) over the previous decade. Over the 1980s the most rapid growth has taken place among the 35 to 44 age group. By 1991 the leading edge of the baby-boom generation — born in 1947 — is 44 years old. Similarly, the slow growing "depression" age group has also aged ten years into the pre-retirement ages. While the tendency towards early retirement has increased, the growth in early retirements has slowed over the 1980s simply because of the lack of many people in these age groups.

There is little information on the youngest age group since the majority are not yet born. Note, however, the dramatic turn-around in this market over the 1980s when compared with the 1970s — from minus 14 per cent to plus 5 per cent, almost a 20 per cent turnaround in growth performance. Teddy bear and toy shops now abound, at least in the large urban centres where the market is large enough to support such operations. But this is *not* due to a reversal in fertility trends, but rather to the bulk of the baby boom entering their prime child-bearing years. Consequently, although on average each baby boomer has fewer children, the large numbers of baby boomers has meant that the number of births has been increasing over the 1980s. This is often referred to as the baby boom echo effect.

This trend will, once again, be reversed over the 1990s as the baby boomers move through their prime child bearing years into the child rearing years and low and declining fertility-rates take over once again as the primary determinant of the number of births. The remaining population growth patterns for the 1990s are already reflected in the growth patterns for the 1970s and 1980s. The large declining growth group is now aged 25 to 34 years and this assists with the declining numbers of births. The most rapidly growing age group is now aged 45 to 54 while the pre-retirement age group is, once again, growing more rapidly than average.

Although the senior age group continues to grow at above average rates, the *rate* of growth is slowing. This reflects the entry of the relatively small "depression" group into the senior age category, especially over the 1990s. Nonetheless, increasing life expectancy ensures ever greater numbers of seniors, and products oriented towards these people can be expected to have extremely good growth potential.

ECONOMIC IMPACT

The economic impact of an aging population has already been alluded to in the previous section. For many food items there are identifiable life-cycle choices. For example, as a person ages, the choice in alcoholic beverages moves from beer to wine to liquor; at the same time, the choice in food moves from beef to chicken to fish. This suggests that in an aging society the demand for beer and beef will decline relatively, while the demand for wine and chicken will rise relatively in the short term and for liquor and fish in the long term. Of course, these demands are also affected by life-style choices, but while major life-style changes may have dramatic short-term effects (such as the reduced demand for salt), the demographic effects are likely to dominate over the long term (as food preparation is adapted to incorporate less salt).

There are some specific demands that the over-40 generation can be identified with, and these products are likely to become even more important in both production and consumption. Health-care products, both goods and services, are one such example; others might be gardening, reading and travel. A favourite avocation of the early-retirement generation is global travel, so as the baby boom gradually enters these age groups around the turn of the century, it is likely that there will be a travel boom. If preferences move that way, and if the increased demands enable the reaping of economies of scale with a consequent lowering of prices, there will be further impetus to this trend. Of course, there may also be disadvantages and increased costs of massive global travel as a result of placing greater pressures on unique and irreplaceable natural and historical environments. A further phenomenon may underlie these changes. The 40s and, especially, the 50s, are low consumption and high savings ages. Child raising is essentially complete, thereby reducing consumption demands, yet real incomes generally remain high, at least relative to consumption. It is in these ages that individuals desire to save for retirement, building up a financial "nest egg" that can be used to generate economic support in the retirement years. Therefore, as the baby-boom generation moves into these age groups it is likely that there will be more saving and less consumption, at least on an individual basis. This means that there will be general dampening pressures on, for example, most retail sectors, especially the food industry. On the other hand, there is likely to be increased demands for qualified financial planners to assist people in the informed management of their increasing financial assets.

This cursory overview shows how an aging population can have a pervasive effect, not only on the goods and services produced, but also on the types of occupations in demand and, ultimately, on macroeconomic performance. The links have not yet been well established, but they undoubtedly exist.

POLITICAL IMPACT

It is a common belief that as we age we become politically more conservative. Some political conservatism may be rooted in attachments to experiences earlier in our lives, including voting for a particular political party. But much may be related to the aging process during which we become less infatuated with "new" ideas and tend to become more committed to a self-reliant viewpoint. This general view of aging challenges another widely held view that electoral change occurs as a result of political conversion. Instead, the aging approach postulates that electoral change occurs as a result of the gradual movement of the electorate through its political life. In an aging population this would suggest gradual movement between parties. Of course, once again there is nothing preventing both processes occurring at the same time, even though the implications are somewhat different.

Other observers might argue that the intensity of party preference may vary throughout life, or that loyalties are dependent on the size of the age group. In the latter view, small groups maintain close loyalties in the hope that they will be able to convince the political system to deliver the desired goods and services, even though they represent a small minority in the population. Still other researchers of electoral change argue that people of all ages are as open to electoral change as anyone, so that virtually any age-based analysis of electoral change will be irrelevant in Canada. Which view is correct?

Political scientist Richard Johnston, in his survey of the literature on this subject and subsequent empirical analyses, reaches some interesting conclusions. According to him, age structures do appear in Canadian party preferences, but, outside Quebec, they are not impressive. However, as voters age, their preferences intensify, although not much. Generational differences in the direction of party preferences are correspondingly weak. Consequently, he concludes that the major source of long-term electoral change is the conversion, rather than the aging of the electorate. Nonetheless, Johnston does point out that changes in the age structure may work through social structure variables, such as urbanization, unionization and religion.

The examination of these hypotheses is conducted through the party of choice, as represented by voting behaviour. Hence, only if political parties were ideologically consistent would this, over time, be an adequate test of conservatism. That is, only if the Progressive Conservative Party always had, politically, the most conservative policies, with the Liberal Party in the middle and the New Democratic Party having the most liberal policies, would it be possible to equate aging and party affiliation with aging and conservatism. This premise would appear to be weak at best, and plainly misleading at worst, in the Canadian political context. The documented weakness of the social foundations of Canadian political parties, and their tendency towards brokerage politics, is likely to interfere with the ideological consistency of their policies.

Consequently, whether Canadians become politically more conservative as they age remains an open issue. At least it seems that age-based analysis of political change in Canada is unlikely to explain why policies are proposed and implemented. On the other hand, although Canadian voters' party commitments are weak and, hence, the electorate appears to be open to mass conversion, this fact alone is also an inadequate explanation of the policy formation and implementation process.

With respect to the senior population, Canadian politicians and policy makers received a clear indication of largely non-partisan age-based politics in 1985 when the federal government of the day proposed a partial de-indexation of Old Age Security payments in its 1985 budget. The strong outcry and co-ordinated opposition from senior citizen groups forced the government to back away from the proposal, and indexation of OAS was retained. This gives a clear signal in the Canadian context that aging may have important policy implications, but that these are unlikely to be focused clearly through partisan party preference.

CONCLUSION

The economic impact of an aging society seems to be more clear-cut than the political impact. Both consumption and saving patterns appear to be related to age, whereas the relationship between age and voting patterns seems to be much less clear in

Canada. This is apparently due in large part to the major political parties' lack of ideological consistency with respect to their
social policies. It does not rule out a relationship between aging
and conservatism, although this too remains an open question.
In this environment it appears likely that the politics of aging
will centre around issues, rather than established political parties.

On the economic side, the trends are clearer. Chicken and fish
are replacing beef as dinner mainstays. Wine and liquor are
replacing beer as the accompanying alcoholic beverage. Salads
are in and are likely to remain so. Reading and up-market travel
are on the increase. The outlook for the performing arts is better
than for professional sports. Gardening is on the increase, and
there are all sorts of niches in the over-40 age groups for the
marketer to work on. Even traditional products like cosmetics
and magazines have to be carefully redefined to meet the requirements of an aging society. These changes are already being
reflected in promotions and advertising.

With the baby boomers beginning to enter their prime personal savings years, financial planners and advisors will be in
increased demand. And capital will become more plentiful to
society. With labour-force growth slowing (see Chapter 2) it can
be expected that the societies of the future will turn to capital to
do many of the tasks currently performed by labour. Automated
bank teller machines, information gathering on the personal
computer and robotics are just some examples currently in
development. Undoubtedly there will be many more. And, of
course, measured labour productivity will show noticeable increases. Managers, workers and politicians of the day will attempt to take credit for this economic success, and the aging
population may be the forgotten bridesmaid, yet again. Or perhaps its time will finally come!

8

SOCIAL SERVICES AND OTHER CONCERNS

A society reflects its values and standards in its social policies and in the consequent distribution of its resources. The issues that will be most affected by the changing age structure of Canada's population have been discussed in some detail. This is of particular concern in view of the aging of the baby-boom generation as it moves into middle age and then late adulthood. They will need to deal not only with the competition and pressures of middle age, but will also need to plan for the conditions in which they will live their later years.

This chapter elaborates on subjects that have been only mentioned briefly so far. It also addresses areas of concern that have not been specifically dealt with in previous chapters.

THE ROLE OF SOCIAL SERVICES

Surveys and data analyses indicate that only 8 per cent of those age 65 and over use the health-care system in any major fashion, and that most older adults consult a family physician at the same rate as younger adults. The usage rate alters only late in life with the increased likelihood of a hospital admission for a terminal illness. Given these facts, it is not surprising that, according to other surveys that have looked at the requirements of the elderly and their informal care-givers, the need is not so much for health services on an ongoing basis, as for social services in the broad sense.

Indeed, with policies to keep older and very old adults in their own homes as long as possible, the need for basic social services will probably increase. Surveys of seniors have indicated that services such as home making, shopping, meal preparation, house maintenance and friendly visiting are currently required by many. The structure of the family is changing due to later marriages, multiple marriages, lower birth rates and the changing role of women. In addition, with increased urbanization, it is necessary to examine the concept of community, and the implications of what is really meant by community-based services. Current policies are based on the apparent desire for the elderly to stay in their own homes as long as possible, and the governmental expectation that it may be less costly if institutional care is postponed or largely made unnecessary. There is, however, the concern that the people, almost exclusively women, who would be expected to deliver the informal care services may not be available because of changing work and marriage patterns. The question then arises: what is meant by community?

Eighty-one per cent of the elderly live in urban areas, and communities in such centres may not necessarily correspond to neighbourhoods. They may not be geographically close and circumscribed, and the term community-based services becomes really a formal-care system delivered to the home. The first models of home care were often medically and professionally oriented, but the current tendency is to develop more social and flexible models to meet the needs for services such as home making, meal preparation, friendly visiting, relief for the informal care-giver and transportation. There is also recognition of the need not only for co-ordination of services, but for an integrated elderly support system. This integration must take place not only in geographically designated areas, but between different levels of care. For instance, institutions and community-based social services, as well as health care, must be integrated so that they are supportive of one another.

Social services will have to face the challenge of assessing the level of need, and, of redefining the most appropriate way of delivering services. The former requires a professional management and supervisory role; the latter, recognition of the fact that important services may be those not usually classified as professional. Many of the necessary services, such as meals-on-wheels, wheels-to-meals, home making, shopping and friendly visiting are currently delivered by volunteers and non-profit, or charitable, organizations. Future changes may require that there be more support for these organizations and the services they deliver. In the case of some services, for example home making, a licensing and bonding procedure, as well as adequate training and recognition, may be necessary to protect the consumer and make the work attractive to appropriate candidates. Future generations of women are less likely to wish to take low paying service jobs, and new immigrants require language and skill training before assuming this important task.

SOCIAL SUPPORTS

While it is clear that families, particularly women as spouses, daughters and daughters-in-law provide a large amount of the informal social services, it is also apparent that this support or network will be less available in the future because of the changing roles of women, the low fertility rate of baby boomers, and the increased rate of divorce. The baby-boom generation may have to depend more on siblings and friends, or on the formal-care system, than on the nuclear family. Older individuals are choosing to live alone, and increasingly prefer what has been referred to as familial relationships characterized by "intimacy at a distance." In recent studies in the United States and Canada geographic distance between parents and their adult children is not too great, usually a ten to fifteen minute drive from at least one family member.

The social network that individuals rely on to meet their needs is, however, only partly family. Friends and individuals who share work or leisure activity are an important resource for gathering necessary information, as well as providing certain types of assistance. The literature suggests that peer relationships of various types are of great importance in promoting high morale and feelings of satisfaction, and it has been shown that people who have broad social networks, which have been developed over their lifetimes, are happier. Previous generations of women and the present elderly tended to lead fairly circumscribed lives and had little opportunity for developing the necessary social skills involved in "networking." However, there are indications that baby boomers, especially women, have become more conscious of, and more dependent on, social contacts. This social capacity, and the social networks established earlier, may prove not only helpful and beneficial, but also necessary in later life.

TRANSPORTATION

It is clear that no matter what activities and facilities are available in the community, availability of transport is crucial. Seniors frequently report problems in transportation since many no longer feel comfortable driving private cars because of greater difficulty in seeing or hearing, or in adapting to changing conditions. While many do drive until late in life, the dependence on public transportation certainly increases with age. However, public transportation is for the most part not well adapted to the elderly or the handicapped. Older people may need more time for embarking and disembarking from vehicles. They have more trouble climbing stairs, or even using escalators. Buses often have a high step to ascend and descend, and schedules may be unpredictable, thereby necessitating considerable waiting, which may be a strain on the elderly. In urban areas, there will be increasing pressure to adapt the system to better service for older people. Innovative systems exist in some places, but more changes will be demanded. At present, even in urban areas, services are often not available in the evenings and weekends. Social services and health-care programmes are usually funded without thought for, or provision of, transportation to and from such centres. Individuals, therefore, may not be able to gain access to services, or may do so only at considerable expense. Currently, moreover, the elderly often depend on volunteers for transportation, a situation that may not be as readily available in the future.

RURAL AND URBAN DIFFERENCES

Although 81 per cent of all adults over 65 live in urban areas, small towns and semi-rural settings have a high proportion of elderly. This is usually the result of younger family members having moved to the urban areas for greater economic opportunity. On the other hand, some retirees move to more rural areas because they enjoy the lower cost of living and more pastoral environments. In very late life, however, when there may be greater dependency, there is a tendency to move to urban areas for services and to be closer to adult children.

In rural and semi-rural areas, friends, kin and neighbours are more available for crisis situations and short-term help, but long-term care tends to be a problem. For transportation, people are usually more dependent on the automobile. Some areas do not have taxi service, or the distances may make taxi service very expensive. Shopping, doctors appointments and even social activities may become more inaccessible and make the older person less mobile and, therefore, more likely to become isolated. Some regions have developed volunteer transportation services, and others have even developed car pools and regionally subsidized systems.

RETIREMENT

While there is considerable literature on such aspects of retirement as income security, health, housing and transportation the social and psychological dimensions are often overlooked. The term "retirement" itself is sometimes a problem since it tends to give rise to the picture of someone literally withdrawing from active involvement in life, rather than only withdrawing from full-time paid employment.

The issue of mandatory retirement has been, and continues to be, the focus of much discussion. Mandatory retirement was originally introduced to provide a mechanism for opening jobs to younger members of society, and to allow for the pension system to provide income to individuals to enable them to withdraw from paid employment to a well-deserved "rest." With the introduction of the Charter of Rights and the emergence of a healthier group of young-old, there has been pressure to develop "flexible" retirement policies. Some provinces of Canada and some institutions have already introduced flexible retirement policies. The impact of these policies on institutions and the work place generally is not yet completely known, but some studies suggest that the majority of people tend to choose early retirement if it is financially attractive and only a small percentage, about 2 per cent, remain in full-time employment after the age of 68. However, with a healthier, better-educated group under greater economic pressure, a greater number may choose to remain in the work-force in future years.

Although individuals often think of planning for financial security, housing and health, they are less likely to plan for changes in dealing with life on a daily basis. Work means different things to different people, and the conditions of their work will affect how they feel. However, for almost everyone, work not only provides an income, but it contributes to a person's identity and self-esteem; it structures time and it offers the opportunity for interacting with other people, forming friendships and sharing interests. Consequently, a person facing retirement has to think about what it will mean to withdraw from the work place. Most individuals handle this transition very well and 70 per cent of retirees report they are happy, and satisfied with their lives. Some say it is the best time ever. However, some, about 30 per cent, experience various degrees of difficulty. Individuals whose jobs offered them significant status may have to seek other opportunities to satisfy their need for recognition. Those whose work and leisure were inseparable may also have to seek outlets for their creativity and productivity, or find ways of using their skills in a somewhat different context.

People also vary in their ability to structure time. Although we may all look forward to the time when our life is not regulated by the clock, as it tends to be during our child rearing and working lives, many retirees find that time hangs heavily on their hands. It is important to find activities or interests that are involving and satisfying. Just keeping busy may not be satisfying, so it is important to find something to care about that is rewarding. It may be a new endeavour, a second career, a hobby, volunteer work — the challenges are endless. Retirees should also make an effort to meet people and to maintain friendships. Having a social network is important, but retirees may have to be more active in maintaining and developing ties with other people.

Single individuals living alone will have a particular need to develop and maintain a social network. Couples will be less vulnerable in this respect, but there could still be strains on the relationship when the pattern of everyday life changes. For this reason it is desirable that communication between couples is open and that mutual understanding and agreement is reached about such things as the need for privacy, the time spent apart on individual interests and the time spent together.

It is difficult to predict how the baby-boom generation will feel about retirement, or even if they will have the options for earlier or later retirement. The present elderly were brought up with a very strong work ethic, whereas today's younger adults and middle-aged put great value on their leisure time. There has been the suggestion that they may opt for earlier retirement. However, it is unclear what economic pressures will exist and whether they will have much choice. There is already some evidence of difficulty baby boomers face in reconciling their desire for leisure with the need to work in a highly competitive situation.

The current very elderly had less opportunity for, and training in, the use of leisure time. But those who are now "young-old" seem to enjoy having the leisure to do many of the things that they could not do in their younger years, and many have the means to indulge themselves in a variety of leisure pursuits. Travel is popular with retirees, and seniors are travelling a great deal, particularly in organized group travel.

VOLUNTEER SERVICE

Volunteers have played an important role in delivering a wide range of social and health services. In the past, young and middle-aged women were the majority of the volunteers. However, with the social changes and increased participation of married women in the work-force, there is some evidence of increased dependence on retirees, particularly recent retirees.

Many retirees feel that society has been good to them and they wish to repay society by carrying out necessary work that really cannot be paid for in the conventional way. Some help their own communities using the skills they have learned over their work life, and others join programmes that help developing countries. There is development also of peer-group support in seniors helping seniors, and seniors helping the community generally. Senior talent banks and intergenerational programmes have seniors using their skills to help others. Seniors are particularly involved in programmes that help slow learners, or learning disabled, emotionally handicapped children or creative children in one-to-one relationships. This is of value to both the older and younger participants.

TECHNOLOGY

This book does not attempt to deal with the complex subject of technology and technological change. The earlier chapter on the labour market pointed out that technological change will affect the work place and career patterns, and also produce an increased need for continuing education. There are indications that the impact may be greatest in jobs that were seen as particularly oriented towards women, such as clerical positions.

It is clear that technological changes will influence the social and economic conditions in which we grow older. As some sectors change, others may reflect such a change. For example, there are some service industries that are beginning to use retirees in their operations because of a shortage of young people willing to take these jobs. An example is the fast food industry, where retirees are replacing the young behind the counters of McDonald's and Wendy's. In Japan it is usual to see older men particularly take lower status service positions after retirement to provide an occupation and supplement income.

Technology of both the complex and more commonplace may become increasingly a part of an environment that will keep older people alive, and well, longer. There may well be a demand not only for high technology procedures such as transplants and elaborate diagnostic procedures, but for barrier- free environments, safety devices and household or personal aids to performing daily talks.

RESEARCH AND TRAINING

Canada is developing a limited database on the social and health conditions of its population over a lifespan. These data are beginning to be available, but the research is not well-supported and there is little reliable information about the over-85 group. There is little evaluation of programmes and services, and insufficient resources devoted to basic research, in the social sciences and the biological and health sciences. Canada's greatest resource is probably its human resources, and a well-educated, technologically sophisticated population is important for our national well-being, as well as for maintaining a competitive edge in world markets. It is imperative that we understand the aging process in the middle to later years of life from an economic, behavioural and biological perspective. This is a multi- and interdisciplinary field and infrastructures should be in place to develop and provide the information society and individuals will need about aging and the aged.

To foster research, education, particularly post-secondary education, is critical. There is also a need for trained personnel in the health- and social-care fields.

DECISION-MAKING AND CHOICES

The issues are wide-ranging and Canadians do not have a long history of organizing around specific issues. Furthermore, although a fairly individualistic society in some areas, it is also a society that has tended to look to government for leadership in health and social programmes. Governments for the most part deal with short-term rather than long-range planning. However, as individuals it is important that we examine the issues, make personal decisions to maximize our opportunities, and think seriously about the kind of society we desire. All this requires an active population, one that wishes to control its own destiny and to influence governmental decision-making. The history of the baby-boom generation suggests that this generation will make choices and will make their decisions known, especially with respect to their later lives. The entry of baby boomers into the over-40 society is likely to have far- reaching and lasting effects.

9

INEVITABLE CHANGES
AND CRITICAL DECISIONS

This book has been concerned with a multitude of issues in a variety of domains — from health to housing and from promotions to pensions. While most people would recognize the importance of these issues for both individual and social planning, it is not always clear if, and how, they are linked. We see demography and, in particular, aging as the common thread found over and over again as a major determinant of past trends and future challenges.

Our focus has been on the over-40 age groups. This takes on particular importance in the late 1980s because the leading edge of the baby-boom generation, born between 1947 and 1966 in Canada, are now entering their 40s. And this is only the leading edge — the influx of the remainder of the massive baby-boom generation will inevitably enter the over-40 age groups over the remainder of the twentieth century, and into the twenty-first century. The sheer size of this generation has had enormous repercussions on society, and it is reasonable to expect these repercussions to continue as baby boomers enter their mature and older years. Of course, their needs and demands will be different, and that is what this book attempts to explore.

There are solid foundations for such explorations. The massive migration of young people to Canada prior to the First World War led, logically, to a growth in the retired population in Canada over the 1960s and 1970s. Then in the 1980s those born in the "Roaring Twenties" started to reach retirement age. This steady increase in both the number and the proportion of the population in the older age brackets has raised the consciousness and responsiveness of society to their special needs — housing, income maintenance, health care — and it is these current discussions and responses (or lack of same) that form the basis for the visions of the future.

Increasing life expectancy, resulting in large part from better nutrition and health care, has resulted in its own special problems and challenges. The increasing numbers and proportion of people over 85 in the population is leading to even more innovative responses as individuals and society face the special problems and challenges of very old age. These issues can only grow in importance in the years ahead. Aging, both individual and national, defines the focus, sets the agenda and orients the discussion and the choices.

THE INDIVIDUAL AND SOCIETY

In many cases the choices open to the individual as a result of aging are vastly different to those open to a society as a result of the same phenomenon. Inevitably, both involve adjustments and resource (dollar) transfers from items no longer needed to those in greater need. However, whereas the individual may wish to choose a particular life-style in later years, that choice may well be circumvented if society has not engaged in sufficient and appropriate planning to facilitate these preferences. Nowhere is that more apparent than in the housing- and health-care options in older age. But it is also just as relevant to those still in their working years when it comes to education and career advancement, or to pensions and income maintenance with respect to the individual retirement decisions.

Each of the issues we have examined has both an individual and a social dimension. No explicit attempt has been made to provide an evenly balanced presentation — usually some of each chapter is devoted to individual choices and challenges, and the remainder is devoted to social choices and challenges. Rather, the material has been presented in a more integrated fashion, with much of the "untangling" being left to the reader. In most cases observations and suggestions indicate aspects which are left largely unexplored in this book but which can provide fertile ground for further elaboration in discussion or additional research.

It is important to recognize at all times the interplay between the individual and the society. Individual attitudes, values and preferences ultimately must be reflected in social decisions, yet these very decisions (or non-decisions) may well constrain the implementation of the desires of the individuals. Nowhere is this interplay clearer than in the "marketplace" for votes. Often it is in this arena that frustrated preferences emerge — a society that is not adequately satisfying the preferences of its members is ripe for political change. Careful monitoring of these preferences by such media as opinion polls is now a regular feature of North American society. Yet monitoring may not always be sufficient — anticipation of future preferences may be just as important. It is for this reason that "leadership" is so frequently discussed as a necessary quality in a successful politician. The party that develops platforms and policies that result in an expansion of the choices available to the individual is likely to gain power (or retain it). The increasing importance of the older (over 40) age groups will mean that greater attention will need be placed on their concerns and needs in the years ahead.

Will society make the choices that best accommodate a population of aging individuals? While by no means a blueprint for change, this book presents the issues where discussion and debate will be necessary, and where tough decisions will have to be made.

PLANNING AND CHOICE

Changes in the age structure of Canada are inevitable, but the consequences of these changes can be modified by confronting the issues, making choices and planning. Over the decade of the 1990s there are many issues that will require attention as a result of aging — employment, education and health care are examples. However, the critical point will occur just after the turn of the century when the baby-boom generation starts to enter their retirement years.

Social change is usually slow, and even twenty years is not a long period as a social planning time-frame. But social policy changes are dependent on political agendas, and Canada's political system is much better adapted for short-range rather than long-range planning, and tends to react to change, not initiate it. The danger in this is that without planning, situations become irreversible and decisions are made under pressures that allow little choice. The democratic process should allow for choices that will result in policies that are supportive of people's welfare over their lifetime.

A political system in which a government has to face the electorate every four to five years finds it difficult to initiate changes that may be unpopular in the short term, but which are necessary in the long term. Nevertheless, in many policy areas — education, health care, social services — a longer term perspective is essential.

BARRIERS TO CHANGE

Change is always difficult, both for individuals and for society. It is a challenge to balance the different needs of a very heterogeneous population at every age level, and in terms of a wide range of needs. Barriers to change exist both in the private sector and in the public sector. The public sector is faced with the dilemma of meeting social needs and expectations and, at the same time, containing government costs and expenditures. Thus, in making changes in a variety of sectors there will be conflicting goals. This is also true in the private sector. In the educational system, for example, it has been argued that, with shrinking enrollments in primary schools, resources should be removed and placed in universities or in the health field. However, educators and the parents of young children will likely resist such a transfer of resources because they will press for smaller classes and better education at the primary level. Their very reasonable argument will be that improved primary education will give children the opportunity to develop into well-educated, technologically advanced adults.

In the health field as well, particular individuals and organizations have a "vested interest" in maintaining control of the field because these individuals and organizations are dependent on a specific structure to maintain income, or gain rewards. For example, to meet, more effectively, the needs of an aging population and contain costs, it is probably necessary to make radical changes to the health-care delivery system. If there is a shift from the emphasis on acute institution-based care and medical treatment to a more social model of long-term, community- based care, professionals such as doctors and nurses as well as the institutions in which they have traditionally practised will feel threatened and may be expected to resist the change. These professions and their institutions have come to feel they "own" certain resources, and their status and economic rewards are linked to this ownership. Major changes in the expectations of professionals in the education, health and social-service sectors may be necessary before major policy changes can be affected.

Programmes for income maintenance may also be faced with similar dilemmas. If pension income is to be a public and private mix, it may be necessary to protect present pension funds for future retirees even if they are oversubscribed. Corporate employers with employer and employee pension funds, or pension funds that are only employer-contributed funds, may see these funds as their property. However, it can be argued that the funds are really benefits earned for future use by employees. There may be resistance to this argument by corporations hoping to withdraw funds from these pension contributions when they are oversubscribed, just as employees in the future may resist having to pay a higher proportion of salary towards their pensions when they are undersubscribed.

Overall, there may be conflict over making choices about whether policies should be based on programmes designed for particular age groups, or for needs of people irrespective of age who share common problems. Although programmes targetted for specific groups run the danger of resulting in some imbalances or favoured treatment, the possibility that needs will not be met adequately or appropriately is more likely. This issue is fundamental and will no doubt be hotly debated as the pressures from various groups increase, particularly if there is a slowing of economic growth and a consequent reduction in revenues. The possibility of severe competition between groups, and even between generations, cannot be dismissed lightly.

Another barrier to change arises over choosing between very different basic approaches to meeting needs. The controversy is between giving individuals direct cash payments, with the assumption that if people have enough money they will be able to pay for services, and meeting needs by cash subsidies to such sectors as housing, health care and education to make them accessible to everyone. For the most part, Canada has chosen the second alternative because of the widespread view that basic services or needs should be met by universal programmes. If Canadians are truly committed to "universality," the choices in regard to minimum and optimal services will have to be faced and debated.

A LAST WORD

The issues are complex and the solutions are not simple. Nor is it evident that one solution is fundamentally "better" than another. The critical issue is that we become a well-informed population aware of the choices open to us. It is going to be increasingly evident that change will be a joint responsibility of the individual and government. An awareness of the issues and choices may then lead to appropriate planning and the putting in place of policies that, without jarring dislocations or intolerable financial burdens, will meet the needs and standards of an aging Canadian society into the twenty-first century.

List of Sources

Chapter 1 -The Context and Meaning of Aging

Brody, J. A. (1982), "Life expectancy and the health of older people," *National Forum*, autumn.

Butler, Robert N. (1969), "The Effects of Medical Health Progress on the Social and Economic Aspects of the Life Cycle," *Industrial Gerontology*, 2: 1-9.

Butler, Robert N. (1975), *Why Survive? Being Old in America*, New York: Harper Row.

Butler, Robert N. and Lewis, Myrna I. (1982), *Aging and Mental Health*, St. Louis, Toronto and London: C.V. Mosley and Co.

Canada, Statistics Canada, *Canada Yearbook 1988*, Ottawa.

Comfort, Alex (1972), *A Good Age*, New York: Simon and Shuster.

Erickson, Erik (1963), "The Eight Ages of Man," in his *Childhood and Society*, 2nd ed. New York: W. Wharton.

Fries, James F. (1981), "Natural death and the compression of morbidity", *New England Journal of Medicine*, 303: 130-135.

Neugarten, Bernice L. (ed.) (1982), *Age or Need? Public Policies for Older People*, Beverly Hills: Sage.

Neugarten, Bernice L. and Dolan, Nancy (1973), "Sociological perspectives on the life cycle," in Paul B. Baltes and K. Warner Schaie (eds.), *Life Span Developmental Psychology: Personality and Socialization*, New York: Academic Press, 53-69.

Shanas, Ethel (1978), *A National Survey of the Aged, Final report to the Administration on Aging*, Washington, D.C., U.S. Department of Health, Education and Welfare.

Willis, S.L.; Bleiszer, R.; and Baltes, P.B. (1981), "Intellectual training in research in aging: Modification of performance on the fluid ability of figural relations," *Journal of Educational Psychology*, 73: 41-50.

Chapter 2 -Labour Market Issues

Bean, C.R.; Layard, P.R.G.; and Nickell, S.J., (1986), "The Rise in Unemployment: A Multi-Country Study," *Economica*, 53: 51-S22.

Denton, F.T.; Feaver, C.H.; and Spencer, B. (1986), "Prospective Aging of the Population and its Implications for the Labour Force and Government Expenditures," *Canadian Journal on Aging*, 5: 75-98.

Driver, M.J. (1985), "Demographic and Societal Factors Affecting the Linear Career Crisis," *Canadian Journal of Administrative Studies*, 2: 245-263.

Dunlop, D.P. (1980), *Mandatory Retirement Policy: A Human Rights Dilemma?* Ottawa: Conference Board of Canada.

Foot, D.K. (1987), "Population Aging and the Canadian Labour Force," *Discussion Paper No.87. A.5* Ottawa: Institute for Research on Public Policy.

Gunderson, M. and Pesando, J.E. (1980), "Eliminating Mandatory Retirement: Economics and Human Rights," *Canadian Public Policy*, 11: 40-53.

Krashinsky, M. (1988), "The Case for Eliminating Mandatory Retirement: Why Economics and Human Rights need not conflict," *Canadian Public Policy*, 14: 40-51.

Malkiel, B.G. (1983), "The Long-Run Economic and Demographic Outlook: Implications for Government Policy and for Human Resource Planning," *Human Resource Planning*, 6: 143-152.

Walsh, D. and Lloyd, A.D., (1987), "Personnel Planning's New Agenda," *American Demographics*, 6: 34-38.

Chapter 3 -Pensions

Calvert, G.N. (1977), *Pensions and Survival: The Coming Crisis of Money and Retirement*, Toronto: MacLean Hunter.

Economic Council of Canada (1979), *One in Three: Pensions for Canadians to 2030*, Ottawa: E.C.C.

Foot, David K. (1982), *Canada's Population Outlook: Demographic Futures and Economic Challenges*, Toronto: James Lorimer & Co. for the C.I.E.P., chapter 4.

Government of Canada (1982), *Better Pensions for Canadians*, Ottawa: Supply and Services Canada.

Myles, John (1984), *Old Age in the Welfare State: The Political Economy of Public Pensions*, Boston: Little, Brown and Co.

Stone, Leroy O. and MacLean, Michael (1979), *Future Income Prospects for Canada's Senior Citizens*, Toronto: Butterworths.

Chapter 4 -Education

Foot, David K. (1981), "A Troubled Future? University Enrollments in Canada and the Provinces", in D.M. Nowlan and R. Bellaire (eds.), *Financing Canadian Universities: For Whom and By Whom?*, Toronto: O.I.S.E. Press.

Foot, David K. (1985), "University Enrollments: Challenging Popular Misconceptions," in David W. Conklin and Thomas J. Courchene (eds.), *Ontario Universities: Access, Operations and Funding*, Toronto: Ontario Economic Council.

Statistics Canada (1979), *From the Sixties to the Eighties: A Statistical Portrait of Canadian Higher Education*, Ottawa: Statistics Canada.

Vanderkamp, John (1984), "University Enrollment in Canada, 1951-83 and Beyond," *Canadian Journal of Higher Education*, 14: 49-62.

Chapter 5 -Health Care

Aging With Limited Health Resources, Proceedings of a Colloquium on Health Care (1987), Ottawa: Ministry of Supply and Services. Sponsored by the Economic Council of Canada.

Chappell, Neena; Strain, Laurel; and Blandford, Audrey (1986), *Aging and Health Care*, Holt Rinehart and Winston of Canada Ltd.

Canadian Medical Association (1987), *Health Care for the Elderly: Today's Challenges, Tomorrow's Options.*

Canadian Mental Health Association (1988), *Mental Health and Aging: Emerging Issues.*

Kane, Robert L, and Kane, Rosalie A. (1985), *A Will and a Way. What the United States Can Learn from Canada About Caring for the Elderly*, New York: Columbia University Press.

Kane, Robert L. and Kane, Rosalie A. (1980), "Alternatives to the Institutional Care of the Elderly: Beyond the Dichotomy," *The Gerontologist*, 20: 249-59.

Ontario, Minister's Advisory Group on Health Promotion (1987), *Health Promotion Matters in Ontario.*

Ontario, Report of the Panel of Health Goals for Ontario (1987), *Health for all Ontario.*

Ontario, Report of the Health Review Panel (1987), *Toward a Shared Direction for Health in Ontario.*

Wilkins, Russ and Adams, Owen (1983), *Healthfulness of Life*, Ottawa: Institute for Research on Public Policy.

Chapter 6 -Housing

Canada Mortgage and Housing Corporation (1987), *Housing Choices for Older Canadians*, Ottawa.

Golant, Stephen (1984), *A Place to Grow Old: The Meaning of Environment in Old Age*, New York: Columbia University Press.

Gutman, Gloria and Blackie, Norman (eds.) (1986), *Aging in Place: Housing Adaptations and Options for Remaining in the Community*, Burnaby, B.C.: The Gerontology Research Centre. Heumann, Lemark and Boldy, Duncan (1982), *Housing for the Elderly: Planning and Policy Formulation in Western Europe and North America*, New York: St. Martin's Press; London: Croom Helm.

Miron, John R. (1988), *Housing in Postwar Canada*, Montreal, Kingston: McGill University Press and Queen's University Press.

Shanas, E. (1979), "The Family as a Support System in Old Age," *The Gerontologist*, 19: 169-174.

Shanas, E. and Maddox, G.L. (1976), "Aging, Health and Organization of Health Resources," in R.H. Binstock and E. Shanas (eds.), *Handbook of Aging and the Social Sciences*, New York: Van Nostrand Reinhold Co., 592-618.

Shanas, E. P.; Townsend, P.; Wedderburn D; Friis, H.; Milhoj, P.; and Stehower, J. (1968), *Old People in Three Industrial Societies*, New York: Atherton Press.

Chapter 7 -Economics and Politics

Burbidge, J.B. and Robb, A.L. (1985), "Evidence on Wealth-Age Profiles in Canadian Cross-Section Data," *Canadian Journal of Economics*, 18: 854-875.

Edmondson, Brad (1987), "Inside the Empty Nest," *American Demographics*, 9: 24-29.

Foot, David K. and Trefler, Daniel (1983), "Life Cycle Saving and Population Aging," University of Toronto, Department of Economics, Working Paper No. 8308.

Gifford, C.G. (1983), "Senior Politics," *Policy Options*, 4: 12-15.

Johnston, Richard (1987), "Political Generations and Electoral Change in Canada," mimeo.

Lazer, William and Shaw, Eric H., "How Older Americans Spend Their Money," *American Demographics*, 9: 36-41.

Chapter 8 -Social Services and Other Concerns

Serward, Shirley (ed.), *The Future of Social Welfare Systems in Canada and the United Kingdom. Proceedings of a Canada/United Kingdom Colloquium, October 17-18, 1986*, Ottawa: Institute for Research on Public Policy.

Ontario, Ministry for Senior Citizens Affairs, Seniors Secretariat (1985), *Elderly Residents in Ontario*.

Marshall, Victor W. (ed.) (1987), *Aging in Canada: Social Perspectives*, 2nd ed. Markham, Ontario: Fitzhenry and Whiteside.

Shanas, E.; Townsend, P.; Wedderburn, D.; Fuis, H.; Milhoj, P.; and Stehower, J. (1968), *Old People in Three Industrial Societies*, New York: Atherton Press.

Wigdor, Blossom T. (ed.) (1987), *Planning Your Retirement*, 2nd ed., Toronto, Ontario: Grosvenor House Press.

Chapter 9 -Inevitable Changes and Critical Decisions

Neugarten, Bernice L. (ed.) (1982), *Age or Need? Public Policies for Older People*, Beverly Hills: Sage. *Aging with Limited Health Resources. Proceedings of a Colloquium on Health Care, May 1986.* Sponsored by the Economic Council of Canada. Ontario: Minister of Supply and Services, 1987.

Estes, Carroll L. (1979), *The Aging Enterprise*, San Francisco: Jossey-Bass Inc.

Evans, R.L. (1984), *Strained Mercy: The Economics of Canadian Health Care*, Toronto, Ontario: Butterworth & Company (Canada) Ltd.